the tragedy is nothing more than
noise, a thud in a winter city, then
silence

mpT
MODERN POETRY
IN TRANSLATION
The best of world poetry

No. 3 2018

© Modern Poetry in Translation 2018 and contributors

ISSN (print) 0969-3572
ISSN (online) 2052-3017
ISBN (print) 978-1-910485-21-7

Editor: Clare Pollard
Managing Editor: Sarah Hesketh
Digital Content Editor: Ed Cottrell
Finance Manager: Deborah De Kock
Design by Jenny Flynn
Cover art by Ilka Mészely
Typesetting by Libanus Press

Printed and bound in Great Britain by Charlesworth Press, Wakefield
For submissions and subscriptions please visit
www.modernpoetryintranslation.com

Modern Poetry in Translation Limited. A Company Limited by Guarantee
Registered in England and Wales, Number 5881603
UK Registered Charity Number 1118223

Supported using public funding by

**ARTS COUNCIL
ENGLAND**

Nederlands
letterenfonds
dutch foundation
for literature

This publication has been made possible with financial support from the
Dutch Foundation for Literature. The Focus on Hungary and Ted Hughes
has also been generously supported by Carol Hughes, Faber and Faber and
the Arvon Foundation.

MODERN POETRY IN TRANSLATION

In a Winter City

CONTENTS

Focus

Reviews

Hungarian poetry has had a huge impact on my writing life. My first attempts at translation were at The Hungarian Translators' House near Lake Balaton, when the British Council paired me with a young Hungarian poet, Anna T Szabo. We have been friends ever since, and during her years editing poetry for *The Hungarian Quarterly* she would often send me literals to work on - from Miklós Radnóti to Tamás Jónás – giving me an education in Hungarian literature. Attila József is one of my great poetic loves, as is János Pilinszky in Ted Hughes' ferocious co-translations with János Csokits, 'burning | In the glass cabinet of the present tense.'

Hungarian poetry had a huge impact on Hughes too – without Pilinszky there could never have been *Crow*. As co-founder of *Modern Poetry in Translation*, Hughes was continually planning a Hungarian issue – the second editorial promised that one was forthcoming featuring Weöres, Pilinszky, Juhász and Csokits, and issues seven and eleven both talk of it as in preparation. In the end it never quite happened (according to the Csokits obituary in *The Guardian* this was 'due to infighting within the Hungarian emigre community'), although Hughes did dash off his remarkable version of the Juhász poem 'The Boy Changed into a Stag Cries out at the Gate of Secrets' when he and co-editor Daniel Weissbort were in Devon considering material for the issue.

This autumn is the 20th anniversary of Ted Hughes' death, and we wanted to mark it in some way. We commissioned three poets – Polly Clark, Tara Bergin and Zaffar Kunial – to write something in response to Hughes' translations. We have a translator of Ted Hughes into Hungarian, Júlia Lázár, part of Arvon's *Ted Hughes Translated* project, talking about the specific challenges of reimagining his 'nuclear syllables' in another language. And we decided that fulfilling Weissbort and Hughes' hopes for a Hungarian issue would be also be a fitting tribute.

There was an enormous response to this call for submissions. Many thanks to all those who spread the word and shared their ideas and contacts, particularly Eniko Leanyvari, Andrew Fentham, George Szirtes, Eszter Krakkó and Diána Vonnák. It is so interesting to see how certain images recur within Hungarian poetry – there were multiple cups of coffee in my inbox, but also, more tellingly, many mirrors and a lot of mist. Academic, artistic and press freedom are under pressure in Hungary. The country is currently in the news as state control increases over civil society, with the government recently announcing that it would close down gender studies courses in universities and impose an 'anti-immigration tax' on the income of organisations supporting migrants. Whilst not always explicitly political, many of these poems meditate on the ideas of home, roots, identity. What if that other you fear is, as Mónika Mesterházi suggests, 'always you'? How can we live comfortably in our bodies, our minds, our histories, our countries?

As Brexit advances in the UK, these Hungarian poets offer up a kind of mirror. Like us, they are trying to find a way through what Ferenc L. Hyross calls this 'extremely simple fog'.

Clare Pollard

SIMONE ATANGANA BEKONO

Translated by David Colmer

Simone Atangana Bekono was born in 1991 and studied creative
writing at Arnhem's ArtEZ University of the Arts, graduating in 2016
with *How the First Sparks Became Visible*, a collection that is at once
mythic and revelatory, epic and personal.

Including both poems and letters, *How the First Sparks Became
Visible* is built up over three sections, with the two poems reproduced
here drawn from the first section, which is made up of six numbered
poems and titled 'friction'. The second section, 'ignition', consists of
two long letters; and the series of poems is concluded in the final
section, 'sparks', with poems numbered VII, VIII and IX.

Atangana Bekono's Dutch is rhythmic and incantatory, with
emotive repetitions and striking images. Although seemingly
driven by autobiographical impulse, the settings and concerns have
a contemporary internationalism and show a wide-ranging
intellectual interest, with references ranging from Yoruba religion
and the Persian poet Rumi to American authors like James Baldwin
and Ta-Nehisi Coates.

Ease of translation is often deceptive and pitfalls can be
unexpected, but Atangana Bekono's poetry seems particularly
amenable to being translated into English. Hopefully this striking
work will soon be available to English readers in its entirety.

From *How the First Sparks Became Visible*

II

Who made the young me sweat in bed
with visions from the psychiatric ward
girls who've grown obsessed with the man
and the touch of the man, and the touch of the woman
that makes them realise they want to be a man

I fear the man and want to eat him up
but I am also scared that he has eaten me up
that I was born in the man's stomach or ribcage or in a toe
but escaping from his body has made me lose mine
I want to eat the man up the way I eat Facebook and installation art
and have for years now eaten up enormous amounts of light shining
    on my face

I hoped to be able to eat the man up
to protect my sisters
but I feel what's left of the man gnawing at my insides
searching for a way out through my womb
my navel, my open mouth

Every millimetre of my body
of my thinking brain
is split into two camps
I am a single whisker fallen onto the chin after an attempt at unification
and the attempt at unification has failed
only my silhouette seems right
I will wash down the drain in the shower or I will crumble
I will drown or suffocate in the woollen jumper removed

Photo: Arnhemse Nieuwe

to facilitate copulation
meanwhile I search for electricity pylons
on which to hang my shrunken body
charge it, fuse it together
because my body is more than just one body

I require a state of being
that will make me unnecessary and all-powerful
I want to build a corridor that leads nowhere
and lock all of my bodies up in it
so they won't harm themselves and each other
so they will be present as a single whole without context to confirm it
billions of cancer cells that established themselves in my father
established themselves in my mother
billions of cancer cells that have established themselves in me
waiting for the right moment
silent in a waiting room

All my poems are quiet and still
my poems have been smeared on the side of the bed
my poems are not poems
I am a puddle of blood seeping through a carpet
that tries to turn systems into words
the systems asked, 'What can you do about it, now you know?'
and I was quiet, deciding to go on holiday

III

I wrote a poem about myself
I wrote five versions of myself that were male,
broken, disembodied and confused

6   SIMONE ATANGANA BEKONA

I wrote myself into the hell of being an artist and left me there to rot away
I wrote beyond myself and came up with a lot of empty words

That the moment of ignition makes or breaks all memories
that context mustn't be added, but has to arise by itself
that I put my father's urn in the fuse box when he slapped my wrist
for my dubious breasts and baffling way of carrying myself
that I only exist as a projection of the brain of a white Western male:
I borrow money from a white Western male I buy toilet paper from a
    white Western male
I am the white Western male's thought experiment

I am lying drunk on a floor and he asks who I am
and I am a version of Kunta Kinte forced into a mould
I feel no bond with my given name

I lie on the floor drunk and see patterns on the ceiling
the boy on the floor next to me is a child I want to acquaint
with my darkest thoughts
to destroy him
to educate him
I am an apelike jazz musician's doll
I am Sylvana, Louwiya, an enormous bum
people pay money to stare at
I can present myself in hundreds of forms

I am a cool afterthought, a drum kit, I am a religious fanatic
with yellow eyeballs and a hoarse-screamed mouth, I am a court jester:
I put on a dress, I put on a flesh-coloured dress
and I am seventy kilos of flesh without a name, language or country
    of origin

a nail-chewing collapsing bleeding anonymous entity
without a concrete goal
all energy and no purpose
I do have a good report
well done well brought up

I am a virus that eats itself due to a lack of matter to feed on
I am the most flesh-coloured dress you can wear
a daring choice
and oiled on a snow-white beach
standing among those hundreds of versions of myself, I ask,
'Are we already on holiday?'
I get no answer.

YASUAKI INOUE

Translated by Katrina Naomi

Yasuaki Inoue is a well-known and highly respected haiku poet in Japan, whose work deserves an international audience. I met Inoue in Kofu, Yamanashi Prefecture, while I was hosted by Professor Michiyo Takano and Yamanashi Prefectural University (YPU). Professor Takano kindly provided a literal translation of a selection of Inoue's haiku. The literal translations were far shorter than the standard 7-5-7 syllable count, so I took some liberties with my versions. Happily, I was able to discuss what I had added with Inoue via an interpreter (thank you, Andrew Houwen). My Japanese grew during my six weeks in Japan but is still extremely limited. Still, I was lucky enough to attend one of Inoue's haiku workshops at YPU. I found that people wrote their haiku very quickly indeed – I was considerably slower – we then had to guess who had written which haiku.

Towards the end of my stay in Japan, I had the opportunity to read with Inoue in one of Kofu's oldest buildings, where he read his haiku in Japanese and I read these English versions. We were accompanied by the famous koto player, Dr Tamaki Ando. Many thanks to Inoue Sensei and to Professor Takano for all of their help. My thanks to Arts Council England's Artists' International Development Fund for a grant which enabled me to travel to Japan, where I met so many inspiring people. It's been a wonderful experience and I'd love to return.

These haiku and other poems written in Japan will be published in a pamphlet, *Typhoon Etiquette*, by Verve Poetry Press in April 2019.

Versions of Yasuaki Inoue's Haiku

Pyres of leaves burning
once again in my garden
blazing in the sun

◆

In the abundance
of autumn a baby cries
like a giant fire

◆

Blue-eyed billy goat
tilting his horns suspicious
of the winter sky

◆

Today it is cold
like a dead person's make-up
the cold is pure white

◆

Step by frozen step
winter comes creeping towards
the naked rock's skin

MARIA TERESA HORTA

Translated by Lesley Saunders

My attraction to Portuguese poetry goes back forty years, to the *New Portuguese Letters* by the Three Marias – Maria Isabel Barreno, Maria Teresa Horta and Maria Velho da Costa. It challenged my sense of what literature could accomplish, formally as well as politically. When, as an older woman, I decided to try translating a few of Maria Teresa Horta's poems, I felt I wanted to meet her. What followed from our meeting was a project to produce an anthology of translations, selected from all Horta's books of poetry – more than twenty over a lifetime's career. The anthology, called *Point of Honour*, is published by Two Rivers Press in April 2019: the two translations in this issue of *MPT* will appear in it.

Horta is an elliptical, allusive and uncompromising writer, with a strong vision of her own work – it is powerful, political, erotically charged, almost visionary. Readers want to hear that original voice insofar as it is possible, the challenge is to make Horta's voice resonate in the very different medium of English. Very little of her work has come over into English, and consequently I see my job as translating her poetry as directly as possible – although not making literal paraphrases which serve mainly to point readers to something that is not quite there. It is a fine balance to find.

The project has been greatly assisted by Ana Raquel Fernandes, an academic at the University of Lisbon and close friend of Horta's, and by Luís Barros, Horta's husband, who have acted as wonderful critical friends and consultants.

A Few Sayings about Women

I

Do not eat from
hunger
nor eat out of fear

Do not keep
secrets
in the trunk with your clothes

II

In your wardrobe
there is no frock
and also no fear

Your teeth
are studying
hunger

The chill in your body
is abating

III

Some talk about woman
and some tell the story of her life

A woman
is like bread

Being born
is a struggle

Some talk
about her eyes
and some tell the story of her belly

Like a deadweight
that drags

Like a country
that's alive

IV
The woman receives
the pitcher

Lets the water receive
her knees

Leaning over the pail
she receives the years whole

Receives the water
in the pitcher

Leaning over the years
the woman receives her life

V

No weeping can answer
the hunger of a shotgun

Nor can any china part
the eyes from their tears

The woman in her house
puts fresh water in the pitcher

And the tilting sunset
puts it in a song

Delirium

There are horses

Horses
and not shadows
that amble through the night
side by side

In the silence
of houses and things
they amble along
keeping in step

My horses of
underwater winds
of sunken cities
and dread

My horses
of flames and limbs
of dislocated backs
who feel for each other

Now tonight
the slow body
of dark does not come
without the echo of trumpets

Which the streets let loose
and drive
deep inside the houses
that give themselves up

Not even death
the fever in disguise
not even death comes now
nor does it steal away

There are horses
in the night
there are horses
my slow horses of sickness

BERTOLT BRECHT

Translated by David Constantine and Tom Kuhn

Bertolt Brecht (1898–1956), well known as a dramatist and a theorist on drama, is also one of Germany's three or four greatest poets. He is abundant, various, and a complete master of poetic forms, many traditional, many of his own devising. He lived through the worst years of the twentieth century, and was always in revolt: first as an anarchist hedonist, then as *poète engagé* against Hitler's fascism. And he was, besides, the author of some of the best love poems in the German language. After the war, choosing to settle in the East rather than the West, he continued to write for a humane socialism, though fully aware that the new GDR, within the Soviet bloc, was falling far short of it. Like many of his generation he defended the bad against what he perceived to be the worse.

Translating the more than 1200 poems that comprise the *Complete Poems of Bertolt Brecht*, to be published by Norton later this year, we knew him to be a poet for our times. He saw the markets treat the working poor as (his word) mince-meat. He was the citizen of a highly civilised country that voted in a champion of barbarism. With his Jewish wife and their children he went into exile, so as not to be murdered. After the war, among millions of displaced persons, he returned to a city in ruins.

The poems we present here are from two distinct periods in Brecht's writing life. David translated the earlier, Tom the later ones.

The Mother's Name

A thing the nurses time after time relate
Of severely wounded men
Is that they become very quiet
And children again.
That all the lads who are sick and in pain
Never forget the patient labour
And for every least kindness shown
Say thanks with strange fervour.
And that quite without cause
Tears will rise up in a man and he groans
A name – and it is
His mother he means.
And indeed at the end as though
All heaven were on call as the light of life leaves them
The dying call for their mothers to come
No matter if the mothers died ten years ago.

1915

Dance Song

Dance, oh dance – in the scant time left
Prance all you can on the dancing floor.
Your feet will soon be too heavy to lift
And a wilted wreath will fall from your thinning hair.
Dance! Dance! – Let your heart leap up!
Make the ground too hot for the soles of your feet!
Nobody knows when the fiddle will stop
And the fiddler drop to the floor dead beat.

Dance, oh dance – this night will not last.
Eyes that shine in the tipsy dance
When dawn looks in at the window aghast
Those eyes, dead-tired, lose their brilliance.
Dance! Dance! Outstare the light!
Light upon light till it all goes black!
Who knows when they'll shut you in the earth out of sight?
Death can tie my hands when they're slack.

Dance, oh dance! – while the red lamps burn
And your young heart still beats against mine
Grey Death squats outside for his turn
And there in the door stands his brother: Pain.
Nobody can have too much dancing and kissing.
No one should save, none should put by –
Who knows when we shall join the missing?
Who knows when we must die?

c. 1918

Christmas Legend

Christmas Eve and we, the poor,
All night long will be sitting here
And the room is cold that we house in
And the wind that blows outside blows in.
Come, dear Lord Jesus, enter too
For truly we have need of you.

We sit around this holy night
Like heathen who never saw the light.
The snow falls cold on these bones of ours.
The snow cannot bear to be out of doors:
Snow, come indoors with us, for sure
They'll not house you in heaven either.

We'll brew up a toddy and then we'll feel
Warmer and easy, body and soul.
We'll brew a hot toddy. Round our thin walls
Blindly some brute beast fumbles.
Quick, beast, come in with us – your kind too
This night has nowhere warm to go.

We'll feed our coats to the fire and so
We'll all be warmer than we are now.
Oh the joists will glow and we shan't freeze
Not till the hour before sunrise.
Come in, dear wind, dear guest, welcome:
Like us, you have no house and home.

1923

Many are in Favour of Order ...

Many are in favour of order. When it's time to eat they spread
A cloth over the table, if they have one, or they wipe
With their hands the crumbs from the table, so long as
Their hands are not too tired. But their table itself stands
And their house stands in a world which is sinking in filth.
Oh, their cupboard may be clean; but at the edge of town
Stands the factory, the bone mill, the bloody
Surplus profit bucket wheel! What is the use
Up to your chin in the shit, in keeping your
Fingernails clean?

1933

The Inquiry

The authorities are conducting an inquiry
So they say. In this city district
People no longer sleep at night.
No one knows who it was
Nor what crime was committed
Everyone is a suspect.
When the people spend their nights sweeping suspicion from their doorsteps
The crimes of the powers that be
Pile up
Unheeded.

1934

Driving Along in a Comfortable Car ...

Driving along in a comfortable car
On a rainy country road
We saw a raggedy man at nightfall
Who waved to us to give him a lift, and gave a deep bow.
We had a roof and we had room and we drove on past
And we heard me say in a surly voice: no
We can't give anyone a lift.
We had gone some distance further, a day's march perhaps
When I suddenly took fright at this voice of mine
This behaviour of mine and this
Whole world.

1937

In Dark Times

They will not say: when the nut tree shook in the wind
But rather: it was when the housepainter trampled the workers
They will not say: when the child skimmed the flat pebble over the rapids
But rather: when the ground was being prepared for great wars.
They will not say: when the woman walked into the room
But rather: when the great powers united against the workers.
But they will not say: the times were dark
But rather: why were their poets silent?

1937

CHRISTOPHER WHYTE

Translated by D Syme-Taylor

Every student of Gaelic begins with the knowledge that the language has been, in the recent past, only barely living. The work of translating a piece of Gaelic literature, whether a recent poem or a song, is to recognise that it is a reinvented language, and therefore young. In Whyte's poem, Gaelic is a new speech, resisting attempts to capture, set under glass, and classify.

In trying to relay my own experience of learning Gaelic – a language familiar to my great-grandparents, but one with which I must be continually reacquainted – I have deliberately aimed towards a more fluid and echoing character, working out the many layerings of meaning in a word, as a student would when working through a lexicon.

Instead of preserving the form of the original poem (save for the final break, that draws us back to the reality of the Gaelic voice), I have presented it in the form of a call and response, imitating the 'waulking' songs of the Outer Hebrides. These songs, at once bawdy and rhythmic as strangely personal and intimate, are literature in their own right; a hidden sweetness.

The Chinese Beetle

There is a particular corner of China, in the south-west,

      not far from the Yunnan mountains,   where a genus of apple can be found

that has such surpassing taste emperors would (long ago)

          fritter away
          all their gold to get them, and serve them up

at feasts and banquets in grand houses. But– they didn't taste like apples,

          not exactly.
          I read that a beetle was to blame,

only found in the trees of that region, which lays its eggs to grow and ripen

          in the apple's core.
          They don't stay long,

but a scent as a miracle spreads through the fruit.

      After the mite   has opened its hatched wings and flown not even a blot or
bruise remains – only an amber gleam

          in the flesh
          of the apple, and a startling savour

that not one out of all the court scholars and gardeners

          could understand.

So I do the same with this language.

MONA ARSHI

After the *Mahabharata*

What can be said about the *Mahabharata* that has not already been written? This most ancient text is three million words long, seven times the length of the Iliad. It's impossible to describe what the *Mahabharata* actually is, but it can be framed as a royal dynastic war with a huge cast of characters. However the drama of the family feud is a small part of what is contained in the epic. The *Mahabharata* gives us lessons in ethics and what it is to be human. It feels as important now as it was when it was written 2,000 years ago.

Women in this epic are empowered with mantras to make children; they can curse the men that spurn them and rob male characters of their virility – utterances even said in jest are binding as legal scriptures. In the foreword to Carole Satyamurti's wonderful retelling of the *Mahabharata* she says: 'The text depicts women with powers and privileges they would seldom have again in Hindu literature. Many of the *Mahabharata* women are a feminist's dream (or a sexist's nightmare)'.

Queen Draupadi is a heroine married to five brothers. She is a survivor – wily, intelligent and disruptive of the normative traditions handed down to us about Indian women. Pollution and shame are huge persecuting characters in the *Mahabharata* – in one of the most distressing scenes Draupadi is effectively gambled away in a game of dice, with her five husbands and so-called protectors watching as she is objectified and humiliated at the Palace. Draupadi pledges not to rebraid her hair until she has washed it in the blood of her persecutors.

It's little wonder that contemporary artists and poets are so drawn to this text, which still vibrates in the human imagination.

Draupadi's Hair

After the disrobing of Draupadi in the
Kaurava's Palace (The Mahabharata)

It was like the first time I closed my eyes
properly, unbidden I opened them again
when I entered the walls of the Old City.
Sorrow heavy – I could barely walk
through the chest high reeds, the women
flinching when they saw my unbound hair.

The smell of the Palace was still in my hair.
They led me to their homes, their eyes
never left me. I was saved by these women.
They found me a place to lie and again
I suffered, fevered for days and sleepwalked
alone around the skein of the Old City.

You may have heard tales of the Old City?
Its breath so toxic I hid in the long hairs
of the bohr tree. Girls pitied me, walked
away shaking their heads, averting their eyes.
I swear I'll never crave anything again.
How to explain to innocents and women?

Pinch out my tears I say to the women:
my anger is a yellow lake, the starved city
can't contain it, when shall I begin again?
Five suns, five brothers, never reach my hair.
The tips of the mountains blind the eyes
of the sky and I need to rehearse and walk.

Long-fingered grief meets me as I walk
around my feathery shadow. The women's
stories flow fast and true, within their eyes
are tiny blessings. I will leave this city,
when the new rain comes and rinses my hair,
soaking the forever sloping stone again.

Look, I've begun to turn porous again.
Mothers tell us to dream corpses that walk
through rice-pale faces and as for my hair –
never speak of it to another woman.
I am a Queen with a song for this city
which jangles under the weight of its eyes.

City-women, help me walk and wear my
delicate risk of wings again, now help
me lift my hair from my eyes.

Draupadi's Terror

Unguarded roof and my elbow bent in the water.
Maybe you hear a mumble from the shadows and
you call out? Or you recognise the smell perhaps
of lychees gently rotting in their crates? Our hands
still tremble as if from a recent dream and we button
our cardigans against it. They say they found hyena bones
in the cup-bearers' cave but hurry past those ghosts
that bloom, don't look beneath your feet.
I will tell you everything if you listen or leave your

mouth open to let the rain in – the leaf lands, the eyelid
closes like a blessing, a blister resurfacing or the sudden
stain of lilac on your baby son's tunic. Wipe your lips
with this, narrow your eyes to squint, as the clouds
meet the trail again like a shadow that spills over and over.

Draupadi's Prophecy

I diluted it having captured it under a glass
        paperweight. I tried stroking, peeling and
screwing it. At some juncture I thought I might

scorch it with a pair of fire-tongs. There was
        nothing to be done but still I mixed alms
with betel juice, horse spit and ate it.

I moved to morphine after Zolpademe and
        small yellows. I tested every variety of nasal spray
and capsicum on my tongue. I used warm

olive oil dropped in real slow into each ear canal.
        I tried Zoroastrians, pundits and preachers,
ayruvedics, heptologists and soothsayers.

During the days I squatted inside cool-
        lipped basins, I hid from it along the fissures
in the dark compounds at night.

Translated by Fouad M. Fouad and Norbert Hirschhorn

The term 'poetry of witness' is close to a cliché, but how else can Fouad M. Fouad – a Syrian poet and physician, displaced from his home in Aleppo, with members of his family missing or killed – testify to the barbarity of the war waged on the Syrian people? We know wars end, but poetry lasts. I know only a little Arabic, while Fouad can recite whole poems from classical Arabic to modern. To translate his poems, Fouad first gave me a word-by-word literal translation. In making the poem into English we then work together (in person and over Skype) to maintain the metaphors and images, and negotiate the exact sense of the lines. Arabic, as an aurally poetic language with echoes from the Qur'an, uses many more words than its equivalent phrase in English. Here we chose not to try for Latinate renderings, but, congruent with the subject, we favoured shorter and sharper Germanic words. Where the poem in Arabic uses internal rhymes we chose to use more consonance.

Fouad and I spent many sessions not only on his work but also in freewheeling discussions of English and Arabic poetry. These enriched both of us.

Facebook as Cemetery

1

with a flickering candle we click
on photos of our beloveds
laughing though dead
we bend over to kiss them
and put myrtle flowers on
the wet soil

after two days
the myrtle will desiccate
and wild grasses grow over their pages
blurring their names

the still trembling candle will again
pass over other beloveds
laughing in death

2
the children die silently
– faceless   bodiless –
like crossing a hallway
on tiptoe
they won't even appear in a poem
or on *breaking news*
well-behaved   anonymous

Gehenna in Syria

why am I here in this pit
in thick darkness
hung to the wall
like meat on a hook
a putrid draft from no window
voices of the dead
groaning from the stones
why am I here in this pit

Aleppo

Where prophecies are shut up in boxes,
and flâneurs loiter from café to café,
drinking bitter coffee –
there ennui rises, stone by stone
and all the old tales uselessly pass the time.
Hail cockroach!
crawling up the table leg:
the waiter flicks you off
with his dirty rag

◆

Between the hours tolling one dawn
and the hours knelling the next
a dark designer casts a cloth
walks back and forth
back and forth
before stabbing his awl through the thick skin

No one stirs,
No one stirs the fetid water.

FRANÇOIS VILLON

Translated by Chris McCabe

What we know of Villon largely comes from his criminal record. He wrote *The Legacy* in 1456, a year after a public fight with a priest, who was killed in the incident. Apparently Villon was acting in self-defence and was acquitted, but in the same year as writing the poem he broke into the College of Navarre stealing five hundred golden écus. He left Paris almost immediately and, if *The Legacy* is to be read biographically (always a mistake), he had also left behind a lover who was treating him badly. *The Legacy* lays out a series of injustices which are completely complicit with any definition of modern alienation. Irony is at the fore of Villon's armour and the poem invents a series of imagined riches – and booby prizes – which he doles out to his friends and enemies.

My translation expands on the original with indulgence. I don't speak French so instead I read about five English translations to get a sense of the shifts in meaning and to try and capture a median wavelength of Villon's style and attitude. My translation techniques involved putting the French into Google translate and drawing on sonics to tease the sound of French into English, running with homophones wherever possible. I've mostly kept to Villon's eight line stanzas, though I broke some of them into fragmented lyrics and prose to align Villon's alienation with a more modernist poetic. For the same reason I have moved Villon's alternating rhymes into slant-rhyme and assonance. My main concern has been in capturing Villon's tone and attitude, a poète maudit long before Rimbaud. The published extract here is roughly the first quarter of the poem, which covers Villon's frustration and anger over his failed love affair.

From *The Legacy*

In the year fourteen fifty-six, dark year,
When I, gent & scholar, François Villon,
Being passable of mind, blue in eye,
Mad for it, keen to be lost in words,
But knowing that one should consider
The legacy of one's abilities
(Ever the rationalist beyond intuition)
In case the SIM is lost in the peg drawer...

In the dead of Christmas, as I say,
In the Betwixtmas lag when nothing's born,
When wisemen toss their gifts to the dogs
And watch the frost sphincter on the glass,
And light cigars to warm their hands,
The urge rose in me to smash & grab
Back my heart from the haunted jail
Where the love I bore was used as bait.

This, then, was how it fell about:
I envisaged her praising the Gods
Who consented to my crash, though she
Gained not a cent from willing them on,
I screamed out to the heavens on every street
Cursed the Gods of thrush & clap,
Begging them to give her what I had:
A Canesten lack for the burn of love.

And why I took it as a sign of love
Her brown eyes rolling my Facebook feed
Until I could taste her with no kiss,
And my anima dried like oil skins in wind,
No sooner was she there than off with white feet
Melting in the hour's fire. So what now?
It is not possible to spark wet tinder,
To pull down the moon with a rusty plough.

That vixen glance of hers killed me off
Like an ongoing busting of my balls,
Nothing I've done deserved this outcome,
She will not ever let this feeling cease
Killing me via castration, there is no cure,
No backup channel, I must break out
For our white sheets she's turned to hot ore
And I'm burning & she will not listen.

With the shit storm brewing I booked
The next Pendolino out from Platitude City
To the town of Anger, so fuck to that!
What else can I do, here I'm nobody,
Outsourced inside my own lifetime.
Her stare could vape me like a pyre.
To cut it short, she should be done for crime,
While I'm sanctified on Cupid's altar.

Her afterimage hard in my pocket
I leave behind a body that appears as I pack:
I'm deranged outside of my senses
At the thought she weaves another's prick,

She hooks his catch straight to her mouth
Where it grows; my herring she throws back.
My head's done in by this shitty business:
For God's sake God end this ballache.

I spurned return for an extra quid,
I need to cut loose and clear the decks,
I've deleted her contact, her name at my tips,
And all the apps and posts she mailed me with.
The only solution to life's scratchcard
Is to mail it to death, my heart voided
In a closed account, a B+B at the Last Resort:
An online grave will be my legacy.

There was a time I could have left this to God,
To the Son & to the Holy Ghost,
To the Mother Mary who never comes to me
Like McCartney wrote, instead I leave my riches
To the name revered on every street,
Most noble Lord Baron Guillaume Villon,
My Ferrari, my business, my island pad,
And the tune of a billion billion billion.

Fact: this woman who I mention
Spat me out like a rind of bacon,
Leaving me dangling beyond joy's jaws,
Locked my heart in a dried-out casket
As the draught of excess burns my thoughts.
Laid out like Chatterton on a bed,
Stress maps its Shoreditch across my face,
I'll download God & put it on her data.

MARTHA MEGA

Translated by Manzanares de la Rosa

Martha Mega is a force of nature; she is one of those poets who never try to impress you with the complexities of language, or the skill of their craft, but captivate you with sheer power. Her poems matter because they are always saying something urgent, something important; they demand to be read. Her recently released poetry book *Vergüenza* covers a very specific set of issues surrounding the complex nature of the female experience in Mexico, a country that every year sets a shameful example when it comes to our treatment of women – according to the UN, in Mexico, an average seven women are killed every day.

'Frontera', however, points to a different struggle. It was inspired by the Transborder Immigrant Tool, a Civil Disobedience performance project created by the Electronic Disturbance Theater (EDT), a mobile-phone technology that provides poetry to immigrants crossing the U.S.–Mexico border while leading them to water caches in the Southern California desert. In 2010, the project caused a firestorm of controversy on the American political scene, and the artists of were investigated by three Republican Congressmen and the FBI Office of Cybercrimes. Martha tackles the violence and the everyday paranoia of the migrant experience, but most importantly, the hopelessness and the harsh conditions of merely existing on the Mexico/U.S border, where words, however good and constructive their intentions might be, are never enough to meet the needs of the people. Poetry might bring some hope, but beautiful language alone won't feed our children. We need actions. And this time, actions that don't involve more killing.

Border

i thought, what would i want from a poem in the desert?
would i want a poem
at all?
one that could maybe serve as a staircase
an alternative to dying of thirst
one that survives at least three weeks without trying any food
that knows what to do when i'm bitten by a snake
or how to locate the northern star and why the fuck
should we know how to locate the northern star
if it's just as lost up there in a desert of bright thorns
as me that knows where i am
what i do not know is where is everything else
i slept beneath the wall
i dreamed of a staircase the biggest
a poem i could follow as a mosquito
on to the next body of water
on to the next body
of anything
as long as it moves
but does not shoot.

Translated by Rosa Walling-Wefelmeyer

Following her death last year, the time seems right for revisiting the life and work of writer and activist Verena Stefan. Born in Switzerland in 1947, Stefan published *Häutungen* (Shedding) in 1975, a text which quickly became a classic in the German feminist movement. Her later poetry, fiction, non-fiction and translations of Adrienne Rich, Monique Wittig and Sande Zeig cemented Stefan's reputation and in 2011 she was featured in *Best European Fiction*. *Häutungen*, from which the extract here is taken, comprises 'autobiographical sketches, poems, dreams and analyses'. This innovative work brought to life its narrator's experiences of 1960s–70s Berlin and pioneered experimental German literature. The text's daily confrontation with bodily alienation and men's violences still has resounding relevance today.

Häutungen's style of poetic and political abstraction from specific encounters attempts to realise Rich's 'dream of a common language' for what Stefan calls women with 'the vague wish to have something to do with each other'. Nevertheless, the text's incoherencies and continual-becomings perhaps problematise any easy identificatory reading. 'Orgasm . . . has squashed sexuality flat', so *Häutungen* initiates a sensuality beyond cis-heteronormative measures of certain bodies in pursuit of certain orgasm. This is a sensuality which responds to the immediate rather than the romantic 'green torrent of birches', which understands both aloneness and its own skin, 'the sensual inquisitive skin, the wanting-to-realise-everything skin'.

From *Shedding*

I am certain by the way
that you once inhabited trees
as I did lakes and rivers.
In my sparking mosshair,
yes, sunenergy broke out.

Your hair fanned out
with the roots, the ground,
the memory of life still stored inside its bark.
Every single dark sinew tautens with survival in the wood.
The twists of trunks, these too you have brought.

Your hands rough wet
as soon as I want to live with you,
not just survive. Unreal leafgreen.
You take shelter in a corner of the bedcover
to dry your hands but also
keep me from your life,
creeping so far away that only woodeyes
can be seen and a brow of little roothairs.

Life in the water is long since past,
emerging onto bare rock.
Murderous marshland all around, no
end in sight. The rock
is too narrow for two, still too
little ground made
for a life above the water,
wisps of mosshair, yes,
suns

you wander through the woods, hair
uprooted, most women
long since exiled
or withered, rotten

few tore themselves away in time

many
      alone

hatching the new world out
we enkindle time
we lay the shadowskin aside
fire breaks out

     I cannot remember anymore,
      how many nights there were during that winter,
now almost two years ago, in which Fenna and I lay together in bed
and – back to back – warmed each other before curling up to sleep.

SAMIRA NEGROUCHE

Translated by Marilyn Hacker

Poetry and Resistance appear as two edges of the same blade on which we tirelessly hone our dignity.

Jean Sénac, 1957

Samira Negrouche is part of a new generation of Francophone Algerian poets: a 'species' thought to be destined for disappearance with the post-revolutionary adoption of Arabic as first language in schools and universities. Still, Francophone Algerian poets and other writers – who 'write in French to tell the French that they are not French,' in Kateb Yacine's mordant phrase – persist in writing, and writing in, through, against a tradition that is wholly theirs. But far from addressing themselves exclusively to the French, their work has a life throughout North and sub-Saharan Africa, in all the Francophone world and, in translation, in South and North America and throughout Europe.

The sequence published here is from *Le Jazz des Oliviers* – a book centered on Africa, on travel, on emigration and immigration, on erotic love. Two Algerian literary 'fathers' haunt the book: the poet Jean Sénac, working-class 'gouari' (European) socialist/anarchist, openly homosexual, murdered in 1973, in what was just as likely a political assassination as a homophobic one, and the poet Djamal Amrani, tortured and then exiled during the Algerian war, who wrote the account of his ordeal before re-establishing himself as a poet (and briefly a diplomat) in Algeria. The title of one sequence, 'Mémoire de père,' dedicated to Amrani, recalls Sénac's unfinished prose work *Ebauche de père* - sketch of a never-known father. Sénac's own 'spiritual father' was Camus, with whom he broke over Camus' reluctance to support the Algerians in the struggle for independence.

But this is not a poem of inheritances, or even of revolt, though an
ongoing, stubborn resistance to state and fundamentalist repression
is implicit in it. This is discreetly but clearly a poem of desire, and
where men are edgily seeking each other on café terraces, the speaker
is seeking a woman, elusive, almost embodied in the cityscape of
Algiers, the casbah, the national theatre, deserted cafés, the final
anonymous and providential street where she is found 'under a tree
that was spared | at a building's entrance on a winter evening'.
Embodied in the city, or embodying it: as the poem is woven, the
city and the beloved merge, until it's not certain if Algiers' own
essence isn't being sought, personified.

Between Scrawls and Sketches

To be swallowed up in you
in half-light
to profane the walls of the national theatre
make your curves moan in the square
Port Saïd

xx

Algiers, men seek each other out on unaesthetic
terraces that smell of sweat and fried potatoes. Breaths
cross, eyes not entirely

xx

descending
it's your corridors, their blue
horizon gaze

departures anticipated and frightened
going down
it's fear in the belly, the genitals
tetanising

xx
poets dispose themselves in the public
squares like timid phantoms and go off
on silent soles

sometimes a trembling hand sketches
a few feverish words

xx
to meet you
in a luminous sheaf
made   of the inaccessible beach
and of you   inconsolable always

boats remember, let themselves
be snatched up by the white hill

xx
my sight
this endless ruin
of disappeared faces
and others
inexpressive, awkward

xx

a muffled humming inhabits
and penetrates me

we live on saying nothing
closing our eyes
walking around backstage
of a deserted
casbah

xx

to roam in you so some tenderness will bud
dreaming from far off of your sunlit port walking
your streets in the wrong direction and finding
you the next day under a tree that was spared
at a building's entrance on a winter evening when
we still persisted between scrawls and sketches

IN A WINTER CITY

Focus on Hungary and Ted Hughes

FERENC L. HYROSS

Translated by JL Williams and Ferenc L. Hyross

I met Ferenc aka Feri at the FISZ-tábor 2017 Poetry Camp in Visegrád, about an hour outside of Budapest on a verdant, castle-topped mountain tucked in a bend in the Danube. Juana Adcock and I were there representing Scotland at the invitation of the brilliant poet and translator Balázs Szőllőssy. Our role was to participate in the translation residency programme that accompanies prose, poetry and translation workshops throughout the week. The motivation of the young people who run FISZ, a vibrant organisation responsible for publishing new poets and infusing energy and intention into a literary community under the shadow of an oppressive political regime, was an inspiration. We spent our days with our partnered poets: reading, discussing and translating one another's work from English originals (written by Juana and myself) and English cribs (created by the Hungarians).

Feri has a very original language for expressing himself and his poems are both metaphysical and personal in a way that unsettles and moves me. When I asked him to talk more about this poem, he spoke of Nietzsche crying out at the cart driver who was beating a fallen horse in the cold, of the philosopher running to embrace the horse's enormous head and neck and weeping in the street.

Weak

islands of ice upstairs, splitting, a
forehead breaking them, behind the
forehead is a body with a belly,
under its fastened door is a
helplessly rustling black heart, tiny
organ. cheekbone on the floor,
jawbone and tiles. it's cold, the
bathwater is freezing on the floor.
meanwhile all that can become a
mirror becomes one, with every
celestial phosphorescent and
almighty blackness within. shapeless
red arms, words, but not mouth-
words. it's the palate calling, crying. it
is asking for horses, mechanical
beings, a messenger to herald the
tragedy that happened here. the
teeth are restless, but not cold. if
they were to shiver they would
knock each other, horses beating
the necks of their kin with their
heads, blowing enraged into the night.
they must be patient. there's an
airplane in the mirror with a girl on
board wearing panties, bra,
sleeping. she's drooling on her
partner's shoulder. he
must not sleep, he is thinking of
horses too, but in a different

context, his own world. he is standing
in a bathroom, hugging the broken
neck of a big black horse. the joint
vapour from their mouths turns into
steam, into extremely simple fog.
the plane, from this point of view, is
smaller than any star, but like a
mountain range, perfect in its totality. this
way the tragedy is nothing more than
noise, a thud in a winter city, then
silence, as you draw your finger
along the mane of the frozen horse.
its gums are bleeding, its eyes begging: 'I'm
cold and I'm weak, graft me with
soul.'

MARGIT KAFFKA

Translated by Mary-Jane Holmes

Margit Kafkka died a hundred years ago and yet what is so striking
about her poetry is how biting and contemporary it feels today, over a
century on. Kaffka believed in a 'new woman' ('új tipusú nő') who
would have the freedom to strive for 'professions, work, love,
creation, battle, action, and learning' and she worked hard to embody
this ideal in her own life as the first female author at the influential
Nyugat Review, a working mother, teacher, novelist and poet.

This poem, written on Hungary's 'Bloody Thursday', a day of
mass demonstration calling for universal suffrage, encapsulates
Kaffka's central preoccupations: her drive for social reform and quest
for gender equality. In free verse, Kaffka appeals to both sexes to
consider a new way forward in this charged moment of hope, weaving
intensely personal experience with detailed outward observation of a
city in protest on a day that would see eight people killed. Although
poets such as Endre Ady and Mihály Babits, male contemporaries of
Kaffka, also wrote about this event, no other work seems to capture
the tension of the moment in the way that Kaffka's repeating images
of sky, soldiers, women and writers have done.

While We Wait for Sunrise, 23rd May 1912

Faltering dawn, the Avenue: a stammer of light. Yesterday's
waiters hover tired, yet a fresh brew steams the air and a single
cloud splits from yellow to blue above the park, above
the boulevard of perfumed girls hurled from the cars of soldiers
changing guard; above the boulevard where night-shift writers,
brains wired to the collateral of words, negotiate silence.

I came here too, in an open-topped car, not dishevelled
from lust or games of desire just sad, and I never saw
the Avenue more clearly, nor the city, its chattels, its faces,
its struggles. 'There's no stop to it now' said a man
I didn't recognise and whose name I've forgotten.

We sat in a pinched corner of that café, watched the forced
smiles of girls cancan in stalls hung with tattered posters,
while we fell in to the cheap bitter taste of coffee,
the recounting of sorrows, juvenile mistakes, those we had lost;
how I'd been so sure my love had once been an inaugurating
verb: a rose, its calyx embroidered beyond the suffocation
of youth's greenhouse – its goodness protected, cherished.

Then he'd come, ripped up the flowerbed as if it was a rotten
stair-rug, a pirate who cared as much for good wine as he did
cheap contraband sold on every street. I wondered if he ever saw
his raids as more than commerce, more than booty? I wondered
if I could rise above this guilt, this nagging sense that I should
be sorry and I knew then I couldn't do it. How much I hated that!
It was this on my mind as dawn appeared, still dazzled by the city's
artificial light, the buzz of waiters running; that cloud – a
        kaleidoscope
breaking over tired soldiers, spent girls, dewy-eyed writers.

'Look' said the stranger, 'one red-tinged cloud ignites another so the world
sloughs its lining – its mantel so bellied, the city's mills creak beneath it.
Surely this is the day all the winter gardens will shatter, release
their crystal treasure, the pent-up breath of our ambition, so tomorrow,

life will be measured in a value greater than the body's weight in blood,
something sacred like the kiss of a whore that quietens that stirring
   for battle'.

I listened to this man sitting beside me yet still can't recall his face, his name
though his words had been so moving. – Dawn, I thought, a blood-stained sky
above the boulevard, its tint mirrored in the pale complexions of those girls,
those haunted soldiers, those fresh-faced pen-pushers. Oh, my sisters,
with your obliging mouths consumed by such beginnings, there's no time
to be ashamed. Sons of my father, my brothers, men, don't you understand?

I said this softly looking into the vigilant beauty of their eyes: 'if a task
needs to be done, don't forget us women. We surrender to our hearts only
because they've become such small dungeons of our destiny where
all we can do is rinse out the fabric of our tears, decorate it with needlepoint
flowers. Help us untie these chains for it is better to charge the enemy
than to give birth in empty houses, pace empty rooms, be afraid.
What makes you think our blood is only good for love, for making hay?
We are our own revolution, so pile the barricades with our carcasses
if you must but men, if anything is going to happen, don't forget to
   take us.'

ENDRE ADY

Translated by Attila Tárnok

It is customary to speak of a cultural period by referring to it by a well-known author's name as a tag or call word. Thus we commonly mark the turn of the 20th century in Hungary as the age of Endre Ady, who became the most celebrated author of his time. Ady hailed from a tiny village in Eastern Hungary but became known in bigger cultural centres: first Zilah, currently part of Romania, by attending grammar school there and publishing his first poem in his teens in a local paper. After grammar school he enrolled at the University of Debrecen as a law student, but never completed his studies. Later he relocated to Nagyvárad (present-day Oradea in Romania) to become a journalist, which occupation he held practically until the end of his life, subsequently in Budapest. Paris, in the early years of the 20th century, attracted an army of young talent. Ady visited seven times, occasionally staying for long periods, and sent dispatches, essays and poems to Hungarian newspapers. Time and again he felt a desire to return to his homeland, yet compared to the lively, youthful art circles of Paris, Hungary seemed backward and conservative to the poet. In 'A Stone Thrown Up, Up', Ady found a natural symbol to describe his inertia, indecision and inability to either enter fully into life in Paris or to stay put in Hungary. Ultimately, he was not able to turn his back on his native culture as, being a writer, he was deeply rooted by his mother tongue.

A Stone Thrown Up, Up

A stone thrown up, up, my tiny land,
Falling back again and again
Your son comes home.

He visits remote steeples one by one,
Feeling dizzy he stumbles in the dust
Of the place where he was born,

Always wanted to flee but he can't,
With Hungarian dreams that descend
And well up again.

I am all yours in my angry state,
Loaded with fond, unfaithful weight:
Hungarian in sorrow.

A stone driven up, up, unwanted
I resemble you, my tiny country
In exemplary form,

And, oh, any intention is vain,
You threw me up and back I came
A hundred times. Finally.

KRISZTINA TÓTH

Translated by Christopher Whyte and George Szirtes
Introduced by Christopher Whyte

In autumn 2006, I attended a poetry reading in the garden of the
Petőfi Literary Museum in the centre of Budapest, just next to the
Károly kert. Petr Borkovec, the Czech poet, whom I had met at a
translation seminar in Crear, Knapdale that summer, was to be
reading. I wanted to hear him. A French language poet from Belgium
also read in tandem with his Hungarian translator, blending oddly
the laddish and the coquettish, and observing rather crassly at one
point that the translations might be saying anything at all as nothing
in this peculiar language made sense to him. Overcoming their initial
awkwardness, the audience responded with good-natured laughter.
At which point a gaunt, dark-haired, tense woman, strikingly
good-looking, mounted the stage and, almost without preamble, read
the poem I translate here. I was bowled over, not just by the imagery,
but by the range of vocabulary, the hallucinatory, haunted mood, and
the somehow pitiless precision with which she recited. The contrast
with the preceding pair could hardly have been greater. When she had
finished, Petr, sitting next to me, leant over and whispered: 'Is she
good?' Despite not understanding a word, Petr's unerring ear had
picked up on the exceptional quality of what we had been listening to.

In the course of that winter I attempted a version in English and
then gave up. Returning to my incomplete draft some twelve years
later, I initially worked as fast as I could, supported by the rhythms of
the metre which had suggested itself. Later I would analyse it and use
the analysis to render the English tighter and more supple. The
Hungarian poem rhymes in couplets, with varying line lengths. While
not reproducing the rhymes, I hoped a strict metrical pattern could
convey the impression of steely overall control which contrasts so
powerfully with the everyday, apparently haphazard, intensely

visionary imagery of the original. Two Hungarian poet friends
checked what I had done, the second, an outstanding translator of
Shakespeare for the stage, in his characteristically relentless and
meticulous fashion. I am grateful to them for several improvements
I was able to introduce.

Rainy Summer

A sentence is haunting me, wordless rectangular mould,
  signs and silence's negative, each other sentence is said there,
if sleep's deeper I grope my way after, can hear nothing else
  as it shrinks the rain to a brief, churning axiom, Einstein's
E equals MC squared, it's so long it goes back
  to Creation, so hollow and deep I can't tell where it ends,
its secret beginning is there in the gas metre cupboard,
  reels twisting in just the same code inside the closed box,
your eyes can be seen there, my son's in it too, a blue river
  it draws me, meandering mirror of glittering sounds,
brilliant rivulet, film on the iris deep inside a cave,
  that sentence where something begins or else finds a sequel –

A sentence is haunting me, wordless rectangular mould,
  in the heart's cavity a cocoon, a wing not unfolded,
a spool speeding on that leads home, long unravelling street,
  mauve skirt flapping high in the wind as you rush past a ditch,
when the wind drops it speaks, the sentence, speaks in the downpour,
  speaks behind speech, hides itself in a face, I can sometimes
hear it close by, just one of its words would suffice me,
  on a sheet where nothing is written just one puckered letter,

where is it, that sentence, I'll sit through a night that's ablaze,
out in the cornfield the lightning keeps missing the point,
I can feel how beyond the embankment it's getting soaked through,
but another sentence, not this one, it's always another –

A sentence is throbbing, a long scar no memory's linked to,
beneath sleep's silken skin it is throbbing, get up now!, get up!
a sentence is haunting me, numb, inarticulate aching,
it does the rounds of my body and wants nothing more,
doesn't want to break off, to endure, to pass on or get born,
a sentence that's soundless, one nobody utters or hears,
the sentence is pealing a tocsin, the heart's bell at night,
hoarse bark of a dog on a chain in a void, gravelled courtyard,
the sentence pulsates like the sea in a ship's fissured hull
in the slippery inlets of sleep it gurgles, get up now!,
without coasts, a summons that twists and twirls in blind waters,
a thin thread of moon that tugs at the seas, a slow drumbeat –

A sentence is hurtling onwards, a long, wordless rhythm,
you can hear how it soughs, how it calls from inside while
you're running
then falls silent when you stop short, jabbering in your chest there,
night and day it is there, the sentence, eternally there
where whirlpools are deepest, it beats in lovemaking, unable
to talk in a body that's endlessly dumb among talkers,
it dances, the sentence, in limbs that are motionless,
singing out loud in your head in a throat that is clenched,
with eyes tightly shut, it runs up the stairs to the landing,
hurtles on up the hill, a panting body, on fire,
a sentence is soaring, flare shot high up into a storm,
at the last post a jockey slumped dead on a black, sweating horse –

A sentence shoots onwards, long motorway in the night,
      shoots on in the heart, in the mist, without finding the sliproad,
it throbs in the sleety rain, in the lightning it flashes,
      between bluish headlights it buzzes, that's fine then! that's fine!
the sentence spins round, blinks a weary eye at sharp bends,
      spins round on the downward slope, still can't get where it wants to,
running late on the slippery night-time highway, the sentence
      shoots past the level-crossing, past passing, through mist
a buzz in the speech of stupefied windscreen wipers,
      petrol pump with no people, sheen of a sump, viscous, oily,
a sentence keeps going, no way to tell where it's headed,
      where it came from, it spins round, the steering-wheel slips from
      its grasp –

A sentence is talking, a wordless rectangular mould,
      water, nowhere to flow, undermining whatever I think,
a sentence that ripples, I hear nothing else any more,
      just this sound in the place of sounds, a dumb cloudburst, the
      sentence
drones where it lurks in the metal brain of the cables,
      like the sea's hidden currents it slithers in dolphins' hides,
a sentence tattooed, sound of waves, of a promise not kept,
      I would follow it wordlessly, leave all my own words behind,
a sentence containing the lack of you and your presence,
      fire language, earth language, speech to which speech is a stranger,
a bodiless body, the sentence, hope hidden and hopeless,
      bright container of secrets dug deep into silence's loess bank -

CW

Ode to Men of Fifty

Where are you now, dear romantic crew,
and where now, where indeed, your typewriters,
their keys clogged with dandruff and wisps of hair -
in what darkness do your hearts still judder
wondering if this booming silence is the end of the matter
or merely halfway there? I checked the size of my ass
in the mirror, and well, it's not what it was,
yet I fervently desire you, whoever you are,
you and you alone,
my darlings of forty going on
fifty, with your backache
and your hair greying as expected
your smile displaying
its rotting canines,
your hands trembling
like your voice on the phone. But you go on living in all those ugly
tiepins, in my entire pin-pricked life,
in every airless love affair,
in every flat and stairwell,
in the full gamut of smells. A fifty year old man is like
a poplar bough, fallen in the street,
fit for the fire, slow to light, that burns with a blue flame,
but willing now and then to shimmer in the autumn bonfire,
present even when invisible,
like the air down in a mine, as in a dream.

GS

KINGA FABÓ

Translated by George Szirtes

Fabó is unusual among contemporary Hungarian poets in having an interest in virtuosic form and using form for intellectual discourse. She has written in this way about feminist themes, like the girdle, not so much in terms of polemic but as a kind of existential oddity. It is the same with her poems about mirrors. The mirror, in her case, is not associated with the traditional themes of vanity, moral truth or even the examined self. The poems are about something more metaphysical, about the reality of what is on either side of the mirror and the dialogue between them. The rhyming and metrical sharpness suggest play and there is indeed a deal of teasing out reality. But, under the teasing and play, there is considerable emotional force. These problems, say the poems, speak to our core not our wit, and are pressing matters, necessary for our sanity. All the more Fabó's background is in linguistics and in the philosophy of language, she has written various essays and studies about hermeneutics and grammar, broadening out to ethics as well as plays and several books of poems. Her first collection, *Anesztézia* (Anaesthesia) appeared in 1988. Her most recent book, *Racun / Poison* (2015) was published in Indonesian and English translation in Jakarta. Her work also appears in various international anthologies.

In an interview with Leslie Tate, she says: 'I always write the same poem... I handle strong, unusual themes in a casual, matter-of-fact manner.'

Mirror Image

A pair of glances intersecting.
Between the two the image dances.
Only between this pair of glances

Do I exist as something seen,
This hook and eye of glance and light
– working down the lines of sight –

that now I flash but then allow
to guide me through the mirror so
that I may glimpse the self that sees.

Continually I catch her eye
through moments to eternities
where they are fixed nor will let go,

not once, because what now divides
later conjoins and reunites
every time the glance invites.

It offers then it borrows back.
It breaks up the continuous flow
between the likeness and the fact

of face itself, the visual field
busted open: face erased
before my very eyes, shame-faced,

so vision itself seeks escape.
Between two pairs of eyes the thread
remains suspended in 'instead'.

It fills my eyes in one brief glance.
It flies home, breaks on broken glass.
Another woman, bold as brass.

No seeing it. It's language only.
Multiple pasts that gather in me,
reflections on which I reflected

but do not constitute a presence.
And yet the thing won't let me be
but drags me back with brutal force.

I'm shackled to my image, held
and harnessed, braked and fully bonded,
obliged into an equipoise

stretched across the frozen sheet
of the mirror as by choice,
like rowers pulling on two oars,

dipping the oars into the fleet
current then dipping out again,
dipping and raising, dipping deep,

while it takes, then renders back
in to and fro: remove, repeat,
urged now to part, now to remain

a constantly repeated item.
compulsive in its come and go:
regress, regress, ad infinitum,

a siren that's forever calling,
that grabs the eye and fiercely holds it
breaking the organ that beholds it.

The spell is broken like a trick.
Mere spectacle. A speck, a glance
the merest chance, a stroke of luck.

ANDRÁS GEREVICH

Translated by Andrew Fentham

The poetry of András Gerevich stages the body as a central concern: the body of a speaker, the bodies of friends or lovers, of strangers; body devotionals or horror; fantasy, nightmare, confession. But even a poem as desperate as 'Lines on the Body', in which the speaker describes being 'built into' a body, refuses the merely corporeal in its persistent drive towards the articulation of wordless states of anxiety and self-loathing. Here is embodiment as the body of the poem becomes taut as the overstuffed subject, 'demanding that I pack it tight'. Elsewhere the body is variously eroticised, fetishised or interrogated. In 'Postcard to Nadás' the body finds its place as analogy for landscape. Here the body is altogether more at peace, a living gesture between two writers.

Lines on the Body

1

My body craves food. Always.
Demanding that I pack it tight,
that I gorge and get everything in.
The joy is in feeling myself
swallow a tangible chunk
of the world. Taking it inside
and swelling up, later, stretching
like I've been guzzling sand.

2

Sometimes my body is concrete-hard,
sometimes it's brittle, or soft as phlegm,
sometimes it reaches bursting point
then others it spreads and slops.
Rub and it puffs up and itches,
stroke and it's damp and sticky.
I constantly shift into somebody else.

3

My body is a well I fell into,
drowning me in its tepid dark,
filling my stomach with sludge.
It swallowed, absorbed me,
a slimy throat to a bottomless pit,
an insatiable gooey vagina.

4

I'm built into my body,
raving like Kelemen the Mason
bricking his wife into a wall,
raising a wall around myself
of discipline and restraint:
a ghost in my own body,
dependent upon my density.

5

I'm always fighting my body.
It has its own life: eating, shitting, fucking,
needing the promise of hugs,

insisting, begging to be pampered
until I hold it, calm it down,
each sought-after pleasure painful
as it ends, pregnant with its own collapse.

6

An achy lust fills the void in me.
I toll like a bell and cave in,
cracks running along
my empty bloated body,
stuffing myself with meat, bread,
swelling but feeling
the painful void grow with me
however much I eat or fuck,
like I've swallowed the universe,
like I'm only alive when expanding.

7

I'm one with my body when running.
It falls apart when I eat,
not feeling, not knowing
where I begin or end,
the world my continuation,
the trees, birds, the animals,
of the same body, part of me.
I eat them all up before they feast
on my helpless fatty body.

8

If thin ice holds me together
it cracks quickly and breaks up.
If sheet ice locks me in
a pick can't break me out,
a trapped dolphin, freezing
into the awful weight of myself.

Postcard to Nádas

The playful Tuscan slopes
are chubby as the Zala hills,
how they look like a body asleep,
a brook dribbling like beads of sweat
between the valley's chest muscles,
towards the Piazza del Campo,
Siena the fluff in the omphalos.

ANDRÁS PETŐCZ

Translated by Andrew Fentham

In 1987, two decades after McLuhan's *The Medium is the Massage*,
András Petőcz began to gather material for *Médium-Art* (Magvető,
1990) and wrote in his introduction that 'the writer himself can
become a "medium"' (trans. George Szirtes). The anthology is a
survey of avant garde Hungarian poetry with a particular focus on
the visual, which Petőcz views as a brass tacks approach, 'the most
basic form of communication'. This supposedly reductive approach
yields sophisticated results. Petőcz is closely associated with the
Magyar Műhely (Hungarian Workshop), a movement of Hungarian
writers split between Budapest and Paris. Their Pest office is the
mezzanine of a two-floor gallery space. *Majdnem minden* (Ister, 2002)
– a collected; roughly *Almost Everything* – sees the poet roam
convincingly between vispo and traditional forms.

you own your own thoughts you own your own thoughts yo
u own your own thoughts you own your own thoughts you o
wn your own thoughts you own your own thoughts you ow
n your own thoughts you own your own thoughts you own y
our own thoughts you own your own thoughts you own you
r own thoughts you own your own thoughts you own your o
wn thoughts you own your own thoughts you own your ow
n thoughts you own your own thoughts you own your own t
houghts you own your own thoughts you own your own tho
ughts you own your own thoughts you own your own thoug
hts you own your own thoughts you own your own thoughts
you own your own thoughts you own your own thoughts yo
u own your own thoughts you own your own thoughts you o
wn your own thoughts you own your own thoughts you ow
n your own thoughts you own your own thoughts you own y
our own thoughts you own your own thoughts you own you
r own thoughts you own your own thoughts you own your o
wn thoughts you own your own thoughts you own your ow
n thoughts you own your own thoughts you own your own t
houghts you own your own thoughts you own your own tho
ughts you own your own thoughts you own your own thoug
hts you own your own thoughts you own your own thoughts

PRAYER

TED HUGHES' NUCLEAR SYLLABLES IN HUNGARIAN

By Júlia Lázár

How to translate words born from silence? How to make them float in space, possibly changing their shape but keeping their direction? How to show them glistening in light for a moment, then let them fall back to silence again?

Prometheus on his Crag was written by Ted Hughes in parallel with the poet's experimental play, *Orghast,* performed in 1971 at the Festival of Arts of Shiraz-Persepolis, directed by Peter Brook. The play drew on light and sound effects, and was based on two ancient languages, classical Greek and Avesta. It was linked in spirit to Calderon who spoke about the interchangeability of life and dream, using no words or some kind of an invented language. It was to change the consciousness of the audience, to examine 'the mental state' (Tom Stoppard) within a sound. Actors from all over the world participating in the performance used this 'new language' of about 2,000 words for communicating with each other.

In contrast, the short pieces of *Prometheus* are composed of existing English words, though they are like clots of blood, disembodied, overcoming gravity, floating in the air. Language beyond language. Enormous weight in weightlessness. No special rhyme or rhythm, yet each word irreplaceable. Human suffering wrapped in an unearthly, dimmed light as if to avoid emotions provoked by violent scenes.

The Hungarian language can recreate this density and silky uniqueness through abstraction, e.g. dropping articles (a word = szó; the wound = seb) or making predicates from adjectives (unutterable = kimondhatatlan), choosing the shortest, toughest words possible ('de' instead of 'csak' = only).

'The vital, immortal wound' - extreme weight in a short line with its double contradiction: vital versus wound and immortal versus wound. 'Sun' and 'navel' like keywords, but no explanation. Birth and death uplifted in space. In Hungarian 'vital' becomes vital necessity = létszükséglet, in a separate clause to gain weight. One word, one short moment of pain and (de)light can represent the whole beauty and threat of the universe. As the Hungarian poet János Pilinszky said: 'he who cheats in words does not simply lose a life-chance, but the chance for confession'.

Do we always cheat when we are not alone? Do we pretend that we are what we are, that our words express what we think and feel? As T. S. Eliot says, there will be time 'to prepare a face to meet the faces that you meet'. Translation is a meeting with a happy or unhappy ending. The chance to confess: open up a channel for interchanging thoughts and feelings. Voice and spirit are matched or not, the challenge gives tension, the tension gives inspiration to create or re-create.

The vital, immortal wound.
One nuclear syllable, bleeding silence.

Absence becomes presence, the enigma almost seems to be cracked before the dimness takes over. Flame becomes 'lángnyelv' (= tongue of flame) in Hungarian to create a more vivid (and infernal) image, while gobbet (= gombóc) uses another set of images visualizing a round shape, that of the sun, uplifting the scene again to heavenly spheres. And helping us to go back to the first line: 'No God – only wind on the flower'. Nem Isten, de szél a virágon. Wind. Flame. Gobbet. Wound. Silence. And then again. Our existence. No less, no more. In words, in two different languages, still beyond language, throbbing in our veins.

From *Prometheus on his Crag*

17

No God – only wind on the flower.

No chains – only sinews, nerves, bones.
And no vulture – only a flame

A word
A bitten out gobbet of sun

Buried behind the navel, unutterable.
The vital, immortal wound.

One nuclear syllable, bleeding silence.

By Ted Hughes

17

Nem Isten, de szél a virágon.

Nem lánc, de ín, ideg, csont.

Nem keselyű, de lángnyelv

Szó
Napból harapott gombóc

A köldök mögé temetve, kimondhatatlan.
Létszükséglet, halhatatlan seb.

Atomnyi szótag, vérző csönd.

Translation by Júlia Lázár

'Prometheus 17' from *Ted Hughes' Collected Poems* (Faber and Faber, 2005). The translation is from *Prometheus on His Crag/Prométheus a sziklán* by Ted Hughes, translated by Júlia Lázár, with an afterword by István Rácz (Syllabux, 2012.)

Translated by Brian McClean and Christopher Whyte
Introduction by Júlia Lázár

The poem 'Sacrifice' was written about the turn of the century, when I had mostly questions about life and no answers at all. It is a retelling of the story of Isaac and Abraham, not long after my father's death. It is also like a ballad - the gaps must be filled in by the reader's imagination. Belief and lack of it, death of soul and rebirth of body, initiation, growing up, love and hate, freedom of spirit – the usual commonplaces; that is, the most important things in life.

'As Crickets' and 'Awakening' came about fifteen years later and hold a mirror up to the 21st century. In the first poem the sound of crickets and a baby try to balance some everyday news, making the poet think about human responsibility. 'Awakening' speaks for itself, and was born from a nauseating scene I repeatedly have seen travelling via my housing estate, reminding me how fragile, priceless and paltry our life is; what blind chance decides where and when we are born, and how difficult it is to fight and change circumstances.

Sacrifice

you take the hatchet, son.

> I'd sooner stay, father.

come on. the sun will soon have set,
no one knows who it forgets or why.

> I'll wait for you up on the hillside, father.
> the birds still cherish us though
> we catch them in our mind's eye.

(my hand recalls
each requisite motion.
the blade is cool, the moss
makes bold. the rock, my face
are motionless.)

> (a tunnel of trees closed
> above. is the infinite
> just endless longing?
> my body knows,
> the knife has stopped.)
> father?

BM

As Crickets

as crickets chirrup, then begin again
while at my side my son goes off to sleep
meaninglessly I try to calculate
what it is that remains to be done

they've captured him... he's killed from jealousy...
later they show a picture of the corpses...
Siamese twins... and the bomb explodes...
black: the rescue team had stepped on him...

however, more than each piece of bad news
the season's sluggish passing troubles me,
not having done a thing today, not having
waged any kind of personal campaign:

all I can do is shudder, watch, be wary,
polish up people, objects, as if I could
wash off a two thousand year old stain,
the crickets chirrup, and the night is fine

CW

Awakening

in the shadow of the tower blocks
on a tattered mattress
a homeless man, awakening,
rubs his eyes

maybe he's pleased the sun is shining
maybe he longs for a dark lair
as Wittgenstein longed for Norway
maybe the soul can't stand the light

the body thirsts for, maybe
he believes reality is
his skin trembling in delight,
forgets he is no less debased

than the other creatures
copulating on the other mattresses

CW

PÉTER ZÁVADA

Translated by Mark Baczoni

'Crimson' is from Péter Závada's second collection of poetry, *Mész*, published in Hungarian in 2015. The poem, and the collection, is part of the poet's effort to process the loss of his mother by suicide when he was still a child. In this collection, Závada mixes the deeply personal with the coldly scientific – the meeting point of emotions and chemical reactions, and the impact they can have on the lives of two people. Here, the tragic sense of loss and mourning is counterbalanced by the dispassion of scientific fact – but there comes a point when the separation of the two is no longer tenable, and they meet, just for a brief, agonising moment.

Crimson

Fear is a spot, mother, a discoloured bit of the brain.
I looked at the world suicide map:
where we live is a continuous chunk of crimson.
It made me think of it again,
though it's been more than twenty years; still,
it's taken me this long to know
that an inland sea has never seen the coast.
(Though the discoloured spots in your brain are
like luminescent algae dyeing crimson
some unfathomable, distant shore.) We go explore
the crimson continents of dismay
and watch the tides of anxiety
fall and rise.
They say it happens most right here
and that in people who've attempted it
the resolve will always leave a mark.
I don't know, mother, but
if the face is a crater that I fill with water

does that make it an inland sea?

AGOTA KRISTOF

Translated by George Szirtes

Few people knew that Kristof (1935-2011) wrote poems in Hungarian, since all her best known works in fiction, including *Le Grand Cahier* (The Notebook) (1986), *La Preuve* (The Proof) (1988) and *Le troiséme mensonge* (The Third Lie) (1991) as well as *L'analphabéte* (The Illiterate) (2004) were written in French, her second language, and published in Switzerland where she emigrated after the failed Uprising of 1956. All those books and others have since been translated into many languages, including English, most recently by CB Editions. Her books – in brutal, clear, burning prose – have won a number of international prizes. In 2016 Editions Zoe of Geneva published *Clous*, a book of her poems, some translated into French from Hungarian. The poems I have translated come from that book though I came across three of them on the web. Editions Zoe kindly gave me permission to translate them.

The poems have something of the clear, stripped-down quality of the prose. I was excited to find them and hope to translate more. In terms of voice she reminds me a little of Pilinszky in his later poems: there is an existential desolation about them, the kind of desolation produced by witnessing war or great destruction, one that leaves people numb and unwilling to indulge in rhetoric or play. The important thing is what lies behind those bare words, behind the shattered windows of language.

Nails

A light grey mist
over life and houses

I was waiting for summer
my eyes full of trees
and leaves to come

what I liked best
about summer was the white dust
the warm dust
littered with dried-out frogs
and insects after several weeks
of no rain

the meadow and the violet coloured feathers growing
in the meadow
birds and dogs with necks exposed
to the sharp-toothed saw of the wind

nails
sharp and blunt
doors locked, bars fixed
across windows going round and round
the way years fly the way death
builds its shelter

The Burglar

Lock all the gates
I will arrive evil and unobserved
my hands pale
not one of those brutal types
neither stupid nor greedy
my hands white and slim
the fine lines of the veins
across my brow and wrists
displayed for your admiration should you
ever have the opportunity to see them
but I will only enter your room
once everyone has left
once everyone is silent
once every bulb of your tasteless chandelier
has gone out

Lock all the gates
I will arrive evil and unobserved
my hands pale
staying maybe for just a few minutes
in gloves dressed in dark clothes
every night inexhaustible
in every house inexhaustible
not one of those brutal types
neither stupid nor greedy
so when you wake in the morning you may count
your money and jewels and nothing will be missing

except this one day of your life.

ZITA IZSÓ

Translated by Tímea Balogh

'Personal Biology' and 'Resemblance' appear in Zita Izsó's third poetry collection, *Éjszakai földet érés* (Nighttime Earth Arrival), forthcoming in 2018. The collection is comprised of poems about refugees fleeing to Europe, juxtaposed with poems about Europeans hiding from Nazi and Soviet soldiers. For the former, Izsó drew from her volunteer experience at Budapest train stations in 2015, when refugees were held in makeshift camps in the stations and surrounding underground passageways before the Hungarian government erected barbwire fences along the Serbian border. The refugee crisis is still a painfully relevant topic in Hungary. A few months ago, the newly re-elected Fidesz party passed a law criminalizing the promotion and support of 'illegal migration,' an intentionally loosely worded document that has left refugee families and those who help or support their cause in virtually any way at risk of persecution. Fidesz ran on an anti-refugee platform during the 2018 elections, winning two-thirds of the country's votes. Izsó's ambitious new collection, however, reminds Hungarians of the persecution and violence they and their relatives faced around WWI and II, drawing links and stoking understanding and empathy for current refugees. Speaking about the collection, Izsó told me it's likely that every Hungarian family has their own stories from the wars, but the stories her grandmother told her from a very young age, about hiding women and girls from soldiers, for instance, always had a tight grip on her imagination. In *Nighttime Earth Arrival*, readers become witness to Izsó's re-imaginings.

Personal Biology

It happened on one of the coldest days of the summer.
I set up a terrarium with the second-graders
that we put a caterpillar in, to observe
the process of a rebirth.
The little boy from Aleppo spoke up,
that's just how the dead buried beneath our three-story house
will rise.

I did not know what to say.
Silence quickly solidified,
like cement poured into a dry riverbed.
To distract them, I decided
we should name the butterfly soon to hatch.
The boy suggested a beautifully strange sounding name.
Much later, I learned it was what the antidepressant
invented for children was called, which by then he had been taking
    for months.

He had not come to school for a while by the time the butterfly
    hatched.
Maybe he realised what he said
would not come true
and he did not want to dishearten the others.

We celebrated a little,
watched the butterfly unfold its wrinkled wings,
and let it outside,
closed the window behind it.

The children watched with twinkling eyes.
I didn't tell them it was still too cold outside,
and that butterfly would soon freeze to death,

wanting them to believe in resurrection a little longer.

Resemblance

At the refugee camp, the people arriving from various countries
awkwardly tried to comfort one another.
Later, they took comfort in the fact
that they didn't have to love each other,
it was enough to pick up two similarly sized rocks from the ground,
and if they ended up far away from each other later on,
and couldn't even recall each other's names,
they'd know there's someone out there with a rock resembling theirs,
with which, no matter how much it hurt not to,
they hadn't hit anyone, hadn't broken a window,
hadn't spoken to, hadn't swaddled,
hadn't broken the head in of the blonde who screamed at them,
they'd simply carried it with them, just like the others.
And as the days went on, they felt the weight of it less and less.

MÁRTON SIMON

Translated by Tímea Balogh

I found Márton Simon's work last summer, when a Hungarian poet friend shared on social media one of his most well-known poems, '3:45 AM', from his first collection, *Dalok a magasföldszintről* (Songs from the High Ground Floor). I fell for the simple images and sparse language Simon uses to express the speaker's love for a lover he deems himself unworthy for. I reached out to Simon about translating the poem, which quickly turned into my translating the collection. We've since developed a close working relationship; Simon himself translates from English to Hungarian, and we often sit down to debate translation choices. It's a gift to work with a writer whose poetic sensibilities and humour so closely resemble my own.

Apart from *Songs*, a few of my translations from his second collection, *Polaroidok* (Polaroids), recently appeared in *Enchanting Verses Literary Review*, while some translations from his forthcoming third collection, *Rókák esküvője* (Fox Wedding), are still awaiting homes. Simon's collections showcase his range in poetic form and style. His approach to universal subjects of heartache and grief in *Songs* is very narrative. *Polaroids* is a collection of one- and two-line poems, influenced by Japanese poetry, which Simon also translates. *Fox Wedding* is a marriage of previous styles, with narrative, listing, and even stream-of-conscious poems. Simon's work is always impressive, but *Songs* will forever be my first love. The timeless themes he tackles with direct language and cold, seasonal images of the city are mesmerising, and often easily carry into English.

Season of Empty Tastes

I'm eating powdered milk and thinking about my mother.
A quiet, weekend morning, you're still sleeping,
I'm walking around. On the other side of the window,
there's a white wall, from here it looks like fog.
I'm planning scrambled eggs, I'm good at that.
I look for my lighter, cigarettes,
while eating powdered milk, I like powdered milk.
Would it taste better if I used olive oil? It doesn't matter.
I step onto the balcony, drinking my coffee black,
all routine, like winter itself.
The salt, the oil wait for me,
but when I look up, I see the wall did become fog,
and behind is the forest from last night's picture,
the one you stared at a long time, cutting our fight short,
practically in place of an answer –
I didn't understand, see, just stood behind you, watched.
The concrete below my feet is cold.
There was a lost animal on the picture, in the milk fog,
and I hope that, like my mother, I'll someday forget this, too. But right now,
the forest is in front of the balcony, last night's picture just developing.
Coffee and ripped pages in my mouth,
my cigarette almost done, I'm about to make breakfast,
I love you, but this isn't a love poem.
This is fresh bread, onions, oil, eggs, order.
I've dreamt this once before, but no,
I don't remember what happens from here. Somebody whispers
in your ear that there's a problem.
This is winter, season of empty tastes,
of fog, to be precise, of where, where's my heart.

MÓNIKA MESTERHÁZI

Translated by Jim Tucker

The following poems are part of a collection that is still looking for a publisher, featuring some of Hungary's most prominent contemporary female poets, and compiled by Eszter Krakkó and Diána Vonnák. Diverse yet bearing important affinities, the poems in the collection (almost fifty) offer insights into life in Hungary today from the perspectives of women in Central Europe in the first two decades of the new millennium.

The poems of Mónika Mesterházi offer an intimacy that dwells in a double-wrapped core: narrative mixed into meditation, often followed by a moment of supreme clarity that sets a poem into a larger human context, almost like a sonnet's closing couplet. The four poems presented here can be taken as consistent examples of this approach. Her narratives, and the messages they convey, are revelatory, not didactic. Indeed this is the difference between great poetry and cliché, and explains why her poems feel so firmly a part of the greater Euro-American tradition.

The kind of empathy that creates the foundation of morality, the ability to tell another's story and locate oneself firmly within it, are here made poignant by the unbridgeable gap between one person and another, between living and dead, between tenderness and violence. Recall how Auden portrays the indifference of nature to the human element in his eulogy for Yeats:

> Far from his illness
> The wolves ran on through the evergreen forests,
> The peasant river was untempted by the fashionable quays.

Now Mesterházi, during a graveyard commemoration of mass violence, where the mourners also must reproach themselves for earlier inaction:

Over the bright expansive sky
in choirs of ordered arcs
the wild geese now were coming home.

Here, in contrast to Auden, Mesterhazi exposes an even more brutal truth: nature is not merely indifferent, but seems to ignore human trauma as it resettles into its familiar ways, ultimately obscuring both the victims of violence and the feelings of those who choose to remember them. This is the poetry of feelings without sentimentality, of human experience amid inhuman forces.

That Other One

That other one, the scoundrel
Who knocks you over in a rush
Who can't make way for your own rush
Who fails to spot you after long absence
Whom you have no wish to see after long absence
Who cannot give you a single hour of his life
Who wants hours of your life for himself
Who forgets your appointments
Who scolds you for forgetting -
That other one is always you

Forgive Me

Forgive me. I did not mean
to shout at you (and not because
I'm trying to get things done, and you
are slowing me down). I just read to you aloud:
'The body of the twelve-kilo boy
took the first 18 rounds of shot'.
And then this... person declares
that even a chicken is cause enough
to kill. They gave him twenty
minutes of airtime, *Councillor* this and
Councillor that. And all you did in your unease
was mess your signature up, and I
screamed at you because if there is one thing
that is holy in this country, it's bureaucracy,
and all you did was ruin an official form
you cannot see, which certifies that
you cannot see. Please understand
I find no fault with you. I love you.
I am so very sorry. Forgive me.

SÁNDOR PETŐFI

Translated by Gabi Reigh

Born on 1 January, 1823, Sándor Petőfi is considered to be Hungary's national poet. His reputation and popularity are due not only to the beauty of his lyric poems, but also to his involvement in Hungary's revolutionary movement. As well as being directly involved in the fight for Hungary's independence from the Austrian empire, Petőfi also became the spiritual father of the 1848 revolution as his poem 'National Song' was recited at public gatherings to rouse the Hungarian people to fight for their freedom.

Like other Romantic poets of his time, Petőfi became fascinated by the lives of rural people and idealised them in his writing. His verse was inspired by ancient forms of expression, its melodic simplicity mirroring the ballads and folk songs of rural Hungary. 'I Would be a Branch' uses natural imagery that recalls the unspoilt pastures of Petőfi's beloved country to create a plea for eternal love.

Poignantly, Petőfi's romantic experiences were always all too brief. His first romance with Csap Etelke ended two months after their first meeting with her death, and his marriage proposal to Mednyanszky Berta was rejected. In 1846, he married Julia Szendrey, but their happiness was short-lived as he died, fighting for Hungarian independence, only three years later, at 26. Petőfi's sacrifice of his life just as he had found romantic fulfillment calls to mind his famous lines:

> Liberty and love
> These two I must have.
> For my love I'll sacrifice
> My life.
> For liberty I'll sacrifice
> My love.

I Would Be a Branch

A branch I'd be, if you would be its bloom,
A bloom I'd be, if you, its dew.
I'd be the dew, if sunlight –
You -
Would love me daily.
My heart, if vaults of darkness you would be
I'd be your morning star,
And even if you'd blaze with mouths of hell
I'd clench you tighter, closer, to my breast.

Three Responses to the Translations of Ted Hughes

POLLY CLARK

Marina

Ted Hughes very much admired the 'simple helpless accuracy' of the literal
translation, in some cases, as with Janos Pilinszky, believing it impossible to better.

The water's slack fist around the moon,
sullen like the cheek of my daughter turned away.
Her feelings ripple with helpless accuracy
over her surface. She longs to transcend them,
be the author of her own translation of herself.
Isn't that what we all wanted back then?
I look back through her into childhood's
smooth clay, dreams rubbed into view
like the thin gleam of a wooden rail
or an ivory ornament with its tortured glow.
As a girl, my face slammed shut upon me.
I became print smashed on paper,
the flex essential in a text gone for good.
To express anything meant ripping me up.
I did that, and let others do it too,
becoming like a marina filled with concrete
with a park planted on top.
Will my daughter escape the world, or me,
making our own brutal version of her,
like a rusty boat chugging its filth
into the simple water?
Upon the water the moon lies bare and vulnerable
like dreams upon the cheek of my daughter
offering herself with the helpless accuracy of the literal version.

Pronounced Chockitch

This poor image of János Csokits' eyes is cut and enlarged from a
photograph taken in Yorkshire around 1977 in which Csokits can be
seen standing between the great Hungarian poet János Pilinszky and
the great English poet Ted Hughes. It was taken not long after Carcanet
had published Pilinszky's *Selected Poems*, a book co-translated by
Hughes and Csokits, and the first collection of Pilinszky's poems to
appear in English. For me, Csokits' elusive stare represents the direct
but hard to make out influence that his translation work had on
Hughes and perhaps on the generations of poets that Hughes has
himself influenced. Csokits' unpronounceable name, usually lodged
unsayable between the names of these two famous poets, serves as
another symbol of his awkward yet vital presence.

It's not uncommon for translators to go unnoticed and even
unnamed. Translation is, as Kate Briggs so brilliantly re-named it, the
'little art'.* Yet the situation with Csokits and Hughes is not so much
about the translator's invisibility as about the complex creative
catalyst that their particular relationship of co-translation became.
It is a catalyst formed largely through trial and error, ignorance,
imperfection, and failure; elements which are, arguably, fundamental
to any creative act.

As is common in relationships of co-translation, Csokits was the
middle-man, whose task was to produce a middle-text: detailed and
reliable English 'literals' of Pilinszky's Hungarian poems, which
Hughes – who didn't speak any Hungarian – could then edit and

re-shape into good English poems. The problem was that Csokits' English was faulty, un-fluent, and broken; it strained for accuracy of meaning above all else, but at the expense of correct grammar and syntax, and because of the process of literal translation, always at the expense of rhyme and metre. His word-for-word versions contained mistakes, gaps, questions, numbers, codes, suggestions, alternatives, dashes, slashes; they were rough, unfinished, simplified, flat, and odd. And because they were all of these things, perhaps ultimately because they sounded slightly *un-English*, they offered a strange and fresh and new language to Hughes; one that he grasped wholeheartedly as a means of representing Pilinszky's post-Holocaust subject matter.

In the hands of a lesser poet, Csokits' literals may not have led to such powerful final versions; as documents in themselves they're not quite as exciting as I make them out to be. Hughes recognised their potential because at the time he was himself experimenting with the notion of literality as liberation; the idea that by simplifying or even violating language you will release it from its literary confines: reunite it with itself, but in a fresher, realer, more authentic form.

There are strong positions in Translation Studies against such methods but now is not the time to explore them. Instead, this is an opportunity to praise the barely decipherable gaze peering out from the centre of a process that helped generate a whole new sound for English poetry. Csokits of the little art died a little death, in Tata, a small town northwest of Budapest, with a broken typewriter for company. He guessed, maybe, the contribution he had made. In a postscript to a note he sent me in 2010, in reply to my request to consult his letters, he wrote: 'I am sorry for this scribble. Hughes used to call my desperate efforts to write or speak correctly his language "your odd English"'.
NOTE: The phrase itself comes from Helen Lowe-Porter, wayward translator of Thomas Mann.

Whose

> Till the weeping mouth surrenders and laughs,
> till the laughing mouth surrenders and weeps.

Whose mouth is biting whose here, Hughes'
or Yehuda's? Both, it says, below
the three couplets, quietly in square lips:
    [TH and Yehuda Amichai].
And how exactly
does a mouth weep? But let's agree,
mouth-one is Weeping and mouth-two is Laughing
and if they are fighting to the end I've quoted
and if your short poem
A Weeping Mouth
was put into English from Hebrew, jointly,
in justified lines, compounded now, another time,
through mine: this [half Muslim] mouth –

    I say this because my son says
    that his Muslim friends say
    he can't be a quarter Muslim,
    but these words that say choose,
    choose, choose, are off stage in a fenced-
    off school playground and have nothing to do
    with your words, and when I say your
    I mean the you
    who wrote of thistles fighting over the same ground,
    their grey-haired end, then their resurrected hues,
    armies that fall and rise till kingdom come
    and the you

who wrote, at first in Hebrew
of a kite high above Jerusalem, shepherded
by a child who's hidden from view,
veiled behind a wall –
then who among the two of you
is more behind
the verbs, the vowels, the *is* and *us*
that cast your parabled mouths
Weeping and Laughing

in this staged fight, this *terrible battle before a silent crowd?*
Dumb as inkless scribes, bracketed in the gods,
terraced eyes stare, huge continents of silence
as each mouth crowishly *tears and bites* the other
mouth, even *smashes* – chews? – *it*, to what one
or both of you call *shreds and bitter blood.*

It goes on. You go on. Till the last word
weeps. At the end the crying mouth stops
fighting. And laughs. The laughing
mouth stops fighting. And cries.
And there you stop. Silent
as shadows, confused
as to whose mouth
whose victory
is whose.

And I've just told my son, Zaphyr – who has
walked over to where I'm sat, and says I should choose

cries, to describe what a mouth does, and not to use
weeps – that I think this mixed-up poem, *Whose,*

that doesn't know how to end and occupies
two sides of one page, has become his. His.

Am I Just a Traveller Who Writes Poetry?

Negative of a Group Photograph, by Azita Ghahreman, translated by Maura Dooley and Elhum Shakerifar, Bloodaxe and the Poetry Translation Centre, 2018

In 'I Unfolded the Earth', the last poem in her collection *Negative of a Group Photograph,* the leading Iranian poet Azita Ghahreman, who has been exiled in Sweden since 2006, wonders: 'Am I just a traveller who writes poetry?' It's a question that the reader intuits might be key to understanding the whole book. After wrestling with the shifting sands of identity in the poems before this, the poet has boiled down her existential enquiry to this question. As will become clear later in this review, it's no coincidence that it contains the word 'poetry' – it's an intractable part of the poet's personality.

In 'I Unfolded the Earth', the speaker concludes that it's 'Not that simple'. She doesn't speak only of actual geographical travel, but also of that on behalf of 'a beloved, in the name of whom I travel the universe, stars, | valleys and deserts'. Who is this beloved? Poetry. Such travel isn't restricted to one poem either. The nature of poetry has been one of Ghahreman's major preoccupations, maybe even her main preoccupation. Poetry helps her to understand her place in the world or, more accurately, the world's place in her.

The title of the collection, *Negative of a Group Photograph,* is intriguing. What exactly is a negative of a group photograph, especially if each of those words is given equal emphasis? Does the poet simply mean a film negative where black becomes white and vice versa? Where things have been turned inside out? The cover features several photographs of what are presumably members of the poet's family in Iran. They invite the reader to think about the title in a literal sense – to consider the cost to the Ghahreman of having to leave them behind.

But the opposite of 'group' is also a solo 'I', suggesting the difficulty Ghahreman may have had in defining the self in exile. In Elhum Shakerifar's foreword we are told: 'Azita's poetry is complex: individual words can have multiple meanings and paradoxes can inflect the logic in her poems'. If the title has various meanings, the title poem reveals even more. In it, the poet is much 'younger than anything | I've ever written', 'younger than my own shadow' – so much so that words are yet to coalesce within her and she is 'the third missing person' in the photograph. That word 'missing' carries a weight that harks back to Shakerifar's assertion in the foreword, and emphasises that Farsi is not a language of exactitude in the way English often is.

Although the poem is ostensibly about Ghahreman's poetic beginnings, it also holds within its small frame the reflection of herself in her daughter, and attests to her mother's influence. Maybe that negative space also holds all the words she'll come to write, as a poet of the hopelessness and restlessness that accompanies forced separation from family and home; that characterises exile and, as a consequence, pervades the poetry. It's an elusive, slippery poem (elsewhere the poet tackles difficult emotions which 'remain concealed within the skin of my poem') even though the vocabulary is simple.

In fact, there is something affectingly authentic about the no-frills tone of the vocabulary and syntax throughout the whole book, though this doesn't mean it doesn't offer up surprises. Readers might wonder how much this is a function of Maura Dooley's translation cleaving to the source language. Whatever one concludes, the poetry is so assuredly from the heart it is hard to mind a line like 'The autumn rains rained and | rained' from the poem 'In the Depths of Time'. Talking of which, the word 'rain' occurs in almost every poem. Rain falls interminably throughout the poet's life, certainly from the first intimations of war – 'that weather of thorns and stones' – in 'Red Bicycle' which opens the collection and recalls her childhood in the Khorasan region of south-eastern Iran. In 'Night Demon', intimations have become the stink of burning books, oppressing everything within its reach, creeping onto empty plates and even 'all the way up to Grandmother's stories'.

Rain isn't the only image repeated across the poems, most of which are no longer than a page. There are many burning books (including a striking image of the poet warming herself by the fire of her own burning books) and 'disconsolate' streets. There are hardly any happy poems, a state of affairs that reaches its apotheosis in the poem 'Prison':

> One step at a time, blindfolded,
> You go down into the dark.
> Deep down over the
> slippery edge of dreams,
> past the sour breath of death,
> unfinished laughter caught in your throat
> now that green uniforms surround you.

Nevertheless, hope persists. 'Prison' ends with: 'I am alive | in poems yet to be sung'.

Who is the mysterious 'you', often referenced but never named? It becomes apparent over the course of the book that it in fact refers to several persons, mainly lovers. The speaker is playing a waiting game for someone named Alex or Gabriel or Hedad in the poem 'Everywhere':

At the dark end of the street, in the pitter-patter of rain,
in torn, wet newspapers
among the stories of war, prostitution and small ads for kittens,
in sonnets of Shakespeare,
or the tenth line of Akhmatova's final poem
in every tatty forgotten novel at the flea market,
in every flower petal pressed between the pages of a book,
in Lorca's songs, where the cypress trees bend low,
when I drink the dregs of every bottle, when I gulp down every glass
I am waiting for you.

Alex or Gabriel or Hedad may or may not be the subject of a
dumping in the spikily vitriolic anti-blazon 'Happy Valentine':

Who told you I love you? I lament to the lilies, Actually, I hate you!
I will fill your rivers with limes, flood your sheets with ink,
I'll draw the devil on your pillow and scare the fish with the horns
and tail I pin on you.

Love, in general, is a costly emotion, as in the poem 'The First Rains of
Spring':

It is better to bustle away,
to be busy with some work or other
and keep love at bay.

Through all trials, it comes back to poetry. Poetry as a place of refuge.
It's a way to make sense, even when it doesn't find a resolution, of who she
should or can be in a world where 'old names are fading away'. Poetry is an
expression of loneliness but also salvation, the antidote to loneliness, as
becomes clear in 'Poem':

In the end it always comes into focus
that moment when Time shifts
and the drowsy words,
so distant that only
their backs could be glimpsed, turn round.

Negative of a Group Photograph, in the end, is an elusive, wily kind of animal. Nevertheless, it's a joy to engage with, and has this reader wanting to return to it again and again.

Dzifa Benson

The Liberatory Potential of Writing

Heroines from Abroad, by Christine Marendon, translated by Ken Cockburn, Carcanet Press, 2018
Subsisters: Selected Poems, by Uljana Wolf, translated by Sophie Seita, Belladonna, 2017

And doesn't the soul of the world
reside in the sequence of leaf and gap?

This quotation from 'After Rainfall', the first poem in *Heroines from Abroad*, is indicative of much of the thinking that occurs in this book about the metaphysical concerns of the individual's relation to nature. There is a sense throughout of the modern human world's growing distance from nature, even while we try to retain or rediscover our innate connection to it. What seems to drive these poems may be glimpsed in the poem 'Anemos', the desire to be or become our natural selves:

To have the freedom to stand in light
and breathe out, is the first and last
of all philosophical movements.

Heroines from Abroad is the first collection of poems by Christine
Marendon to be published in English, translated from the German by
poet and literary translator Ken Cockburn. The German and English
versions of each poem are given on facing pages, German first. Each
translation takes a similar shape to the original and adheres closely to
punctuation and even some line breaks. The overall impression created
is one of a conventional meticulous translation, in which the reader may
feel secure. This is quite different to the Wolf book's idea of translation,
as we'll see later.

'After Rainfall' seems to be about identifying a kind of soul or
soulfulness in the sequences and structures that are already within
nature, rather than imposing our own human structures. The poem
mixes registers between elemental primal nouns such as soul, sky, earth
and tree with the specific formal language of bureaucracy and industry
(e.g. Global Office for Building, conveyor belts). This conflict between
registers is echoed elsewhere in too, and partially disrupts our sense, in
small moments, of a straightforward nature lyric.

The poems are mostly in free verse that runs sentences across
multiple lines, ending one sentence in the middle of a line and letting
the next propel us over a new line break. They are almost all regularly
punctuated, with some rhyme formed internally. The effect created is of
organic thought building into realisations rather than pronouncements,
for example here from 'Rotunda':

Tomorrow you set out again,
for the ring-road, where the solderers'
kettles sit on fires and boiled
heart is offered as a delicacy.

At times elusive, but built around moments and strong images, *Heroines From Abroad* is most concerned, as seen in 'Mutable' quoted below, with reflecting this state of the self being a part of nature and trying to write the natural world, whilst simultaneously feeling cut off from it.

> The idea of one's
> self is like that of the animals. Land is the concept
> we pay for, which has become so alien to us
> we soon reach a border.

The borders, such as there are, in Uljana Wolf's book *Subsisters* (translated from the German by Cambridge-based artist and translator Sophie Seita) are more like linguistic artefacts to be pushed aside as the text dances exuberantly forwards. Disruption of the reader's faith in translation and language is active and constant, working in defence of 'the process of translation as an artistic act' (from the Introduction). The translator's role here is one of creative collaboration rather than a form of transcription, and it is stated explicitly in the Afterword that Wolf's poetry 'cannot be seen outside her work as a translator', something very much borne out by the poems.

> we wanted to lean over this phrase like a charted city, to make a point,
> create a mouthspace, myth of hear or say: hier, in this net of tongues,
> one path was well-sprung, a mistake, mystique.

This quotation from 'Can You Show Me On Se Mappe' gives a hint of the text's playfulness, the way it intermingles German and English words together, and the fundamental preoccupation with language. Later in the same piece we have: 'you are here, ich bin wer, a game of routes, but whatever we said the words did not arrive.' Language is explored as a game, one in which the received rules are inhibitors rather than necessary or even useful structures.

Each poem here feels worthy of scrutiny at length. In 'Dancing Double Speech' we feel the exploration of bilingualism or multilingualism reflected viscerally in the poem's 'lengevitch' or language, with its scampering 'word-rabbits':

i went to the tingel-tangel to angle lengevitch. in the cloak-roam every woman received a twin language with identical clothes, a dabbling double. but the mirrors showed only one of us–i gulped: cold spit, spooky skit.

The additional texts which surround the poems, an introduction at the start and several texts on different translations at the end, settle our focus on the act of translation itself. The same could be said of the decision to display the English pieces ahead of the German, reflecting their importance as creative works.

There are wider discourses to be had around the uses and limitations of language, and many of these are also touched upon. The poem 'On Classification In Language, A Feeble Reader' engages with language's implications for gender and gender definitions:

the bending of our gender words began early as a set of pines near coastal dunes – lithe with level roots, androgynously grown... we were more whorls than girls, you twirled me until my needles kneaded veins, compact, compass. which way did they point.

Language is examined and played with again and again in different ways, harkening to fairytales and folk language, and looking at way young children's language develops, before society has a chance to inflict systems of language upon us. Early language is imagined in 'Babeltrack' as:

a babble phase, in which words of all languages are imaginable, a smelt-speak or schmelzing of, a lengevitch, then that's the shore of it

The book is well paced in terms of balancing its more and less challenging parts, each section markedly different to the one preceding it. There are moments of confusion, but as part of a strategy of deliberate disruption, and the book is all the richer and more thought-provoking for it. It does not fall short of the epigraph from Myung Mi Kim which precedes the Afterword, and identifies particular processes of translation as a way to augment the great 'liberatory potential of writing'.

Chrissy Williams

Sight Lashed By Vision

Benjamin Fondane's Ulysses, by Benjamin Fondane, translated by Nathaniel Rudavsky-Brody, Syracuse University Press, 2017

Until recently, the work of Benjamin Fondane was hardly known to English-speaking audiences. *Cinepoems and Others* (edited by Leonard Schwartz, New York Review of Books, 2016) was the first book-length translation of Fondane's poems to appear in English, 72 years after he was murdered in Auschwitz. It can only astonish new readers of his poetry that this voice has been so little-known for so long: passionate, ironic, unrestrained and ever aware of the delicate equilibrium between life and death, Fondane's preoccupations of the years leading up to and during World War II continue to be remarkably relevant today.

A Romanian Jew from Moldavia, Fondane (or Fundoianu; born Benjamin Wechsler in 1898) was deeply involved from his teenage years in Jewish and Romanian cultural circles. From 1919, he was a key figure in Bucharest's avant-garde milieu, especially in poetry and theatre. Fondane moved to Paris in 1923 and was involved with the Surrealists, although he later parted ways with them. He was friends with figures such as Constantin Brâncuşi and Man Ray, who photographed him. His chief mentor was Lev Shestov, the Russian existentialist philosopher. Shestov profoundly influenced Fondane's own philosophical writings on subjects such as the critique of rationalism. A polymath, Fondane was also involved in cinema and even travelled to Argentina to direct a film. His varied and irrepressible existence ended terribly when in 1944 he was interned at Drancy and then deported to Auschwitz, probably along with his sister Line.

French was not Fondane's first language, but his command of it is beautifully fluent and creative. It is hard to classify his verse, which was influenced by Romanticism as well as Surrealist and Symbolist poetry. *Ulysses* was just one of his sequences or long poems about experiences of travel, displacement and emigration, the others being *The Sorrow of Ghosts, Exodus: Super Flumina Babylonis* and *Titanic*. His last poems were mostly shorter lyrics.

Ulysses is a lengthy sequence of 39 numbered sections of varying lengths (from just a few lines to several pages), preceded by two unnumbered sections and a Preface. It was first published in 1933, but after his time in the French army and as a prisoner of war in 1940, Fondane continued to revise it. This book contains the second version. Although this version was unfinished at the time of his death, Fondane saw it as a truer reflection of his own obsessions and of events and currents in the wider world. In the excellent

Translator's Introduction, Nathaniel Rudavsky-Brody quotes from a note by Fondane found attached to one of the last drafts of *Ulysses*: 'here the universal meets the particular, and action turns out to be no less than the sister of the dream. [...] Unfortunately, current events were brutally imposed on these images'. *Ulysses* is an emotional, often painfully unfiltered travelogue, inspired by Fondane's trips to Argentina (where he directed the now lost film, *Tararira*) and by the mythic voyages of the original Ulysses. 'A Jew, naturally you were a Jew, Ulysses', says Fondane wryly, early on in the work. But the sequence also passes through time zones, as well as mental and emotional states from exaltation to despair. Writing of 'those peasants in 1914', Fondane describes:

> the war went on so long, the shipwreck infinite,
> that suddenly men thronged the roads
> drunk on some expanse that slipped
> around their necks like a rope, and pulled.

This is characteristic of Fondane's imagery: strange, almost a mixed metaphor, and stark, it contains both the hope of freedom and the reality of despair. The poet also touches on his childhood: 'town of small Jews suspended in the air [...] I sang all that, but wanted to leave' and writes poignantly of Jewish and family experience, of the long experience of displacement:

> ...My father, asleep in the ground,
> eyes open in the grave,
> do you know it's better under your stone?
> – Here the earth is all water and wave.

They took our fingerprints
throughout the earth and farther.
What's the use of sobs and complaints?
The road goes on and on.

Some sections are addressed to Fondane's family members and
contemporaries. The poem's dedication is 'for Armand Pascal, in
death'. Armand Pascal was Fondane's brother-in-law, and the two men
had also worked together in Romanian theatre. With strong affection
and surprising imagery, Fondane writes to Pascal:

Armand, your ashes are so heavy in my suitcase.

Here is your vast life, that blew the bridges to the sky.

The section most closely linked to family and Jewish identity is
dedicated to his sister Line. A passage on 'the salty, supple, infertile
Ocean' is for his wife Geneviève, and a section on Argentina is
dedicated to Victoria Ocampo, an important Argentinian writer
and Fondane's friend. One of the most passionate passages is for
Lev Shestov:

Sight that sees but is not lashed by vision means nothing,
that sees but cannot bite straight to the world

Fondane's vision often disturbs and subverts. He craves life, but
death is there too like a life-force:

Death was somnolent, forgetful,
forgotten sheet of water deep in the soul –

and SUDDENLY it was there, it flowed in me
like living milk in a woman's breast.

Rudavsky-Brody's translation is hard to fault. There is no sense
that the translator is trying to dominate the translation, and
Fondane's voice comes through very clearly. English-only readers will
find the translation very readable, with occasional moments of
awkwardness, but those who read French as well will find that many
of these are Fondane's own idiosyncrasies (and often surprising
felicities). Whether because *Ulysses* was still unfinished, or because of
Fondane's own raw lyricism, there is a roughness to many passages
which, commendably, Rudavsky-Brody has not tried to smooth over.
Ulysses is mostly written in free verse: any rhyme and metre is
unstable and changeable, perhaps like the speaker's perceptions. The
occasional rhymed couplets and other loose rhyme schemes are
reproduced in the translation only where it can be done with no strain
on the meaning or where the English words are very similar to the
French.

   Ulysses is not just a fragment of one man's experiences before and
during the war. Its themes of upheaval, wanderlust, statelessness and
the sheer force of individual experience are still ours today, and we
can hope that this translation will open up Fondane's world to wider
audiences of readers and translators.

Clarissa Aykroyd

NOTES ON CONTRIBUTORS

CLARISSA AYKROYD grew up in Canada and lives in London, where she works as a publisher. Her poetry has appeared in international journals, and twice been nominated for a Pushcart Prize. www.thestoneandthestar.blogspot.co.uk

ENDRE ADY (1877–1919) was a symbolist poet and writer. An influential figure in early 20th century Hungary, he introduced a modern voice in his poetry. He died of syphilis aged 41.

MONA ARSHI's debut collection *Small Hands* won the Forward Prize for best first collection in 2015. Her second collection will be published by Pavilion Poetry in Spring 2019.

MARK BACZONI translates from Hungarian and French. He was born in Budapest and grew up in London. He studied at Cambridge and currently lives in Budapest.

TÍMEA BALOGH is a Hungarian-American writer and translator. A 2017 ALTA Travel Fellow, her translations have appeared in *The Offing*, *Two Lines Journal*, *Arkansas International*, and elsewhere. Tweet her at @timearozalia.

SIMONE ATANGANA BEKONO's creative writing graduating collection was reissued by Literary Production House Wintertuin and Lebowski Publishers in 2017 and won Belgium's 2018 Poetry Debut Prize on the Sea. She is working on her first novel.

DZIFA BENSON is a poet and dramatist currently studying for an MA in Text & Performance at RADA and Birkbeck College. The intersections between art, science, the body and ritual animate her practice which she explores through poetry, theatre, storytelling and journalism.

TARA BERGIN has written extensively on the topic of poetic translation, including two chapters in *Ted Hughes in Context* (Cambridge University Press). Her second poetry collection *The Tragic Death of Eleanor Marx* was published by Carcanet last year.

BERTOLT BRECHT (1898–1956), well known as a dramatist and theorist on drama, was also one of Germany's three or four greatest poets.

POLLY CLARK is a poet and novelist. Her latest work is *Larchfield*, a novel inspired by WH Auden's life as a schoolmaster in Helensburgh, Scotland, where he wrote *The Orators*.

DAVID COLMER is a prize-winning translator of mainly Dutch literature. Recent publications include Paul van Ostaijen's *Occupied City* and Menno Wigman's *Window-cleaner Sees Paintings*.

DAVID CONSTANTINE taught German at Queen's College, Oxford. He is now a freelance writer and translator. With his wife Helen he edited *MPT* 2003–12.

KINGA FABÓ (b. 1953) is a poet and essayist with an interest in form and in poetry as a kind of metaphysical debate. She has published several book, most recently *Poison* (2015)

ANDREW FENTHAM was awarded 2nd place in the 2017 Stephen Spender Prize for a translation from the Hungarian of András Gerevich. *Romanesco* (Eyewear) also appeared last year. This year he launched The Grammarsow, a residency project in Cornwall for Scottish poets, in the footsteps of WS Graham. www.thegrammarsow.co.uk

FOUAD M. FOUAD is a physician-poet from Aleppo. He and his family left Syria in 2012. He is now at the American University of Beirut. He has published five collections of poetry in Arabic.

ANDRÁS GEREVICH has published four books of poetry and translated writers including Seamus Heaney, Frank O'Hara and David Lynch into Hungarian. He is a former president of the József Attila Kör and has been awarded several international scholarships and residencies.

MARILYN HACKER is the author of thirteen books of poems. Her translations include books by Marie Etienne, Vénus Khoury-Ghata, Habib Tengour, Rachida Madani and Emmanuel Moses' *Preludes and Fugues*.

NORBERT HIRSCHHORN is an international public health physician, an American settled in the UK, and proud to follow in the tradition of physician-poets. He has published five collections of poetry. See www.bertzpoet.com.

MARY-JANE HOLMES is chief editor at *Fish Publishing*, consulting editor at *The Well Review* and guest editor at *V.Press*. Her debut poetry collection *Heliotrope with Matches and Magnifying Glass* features translations of Argentinian poet Alfonsina Storni.

MARIA TERESA HORTA, one of the most revered writers of modern Portugal, began writing before the revolution; her latest volume came out in 2018. Now in her 80s, she continues to give public readings.

TED HUGHES was an English poet. He co-founded *Modern Poetry in Translation* with Daniel Weissbort, and was an influential translator of Pilinszky, Ovid and many others.

FERENC L. HYROSS is a Hungarian poet of the younger generation. He recently published his first collection, *Tömegvonzás* (FISZ).

YASUAKE INOUE has been editor and president of the haiku society Kakko (Cuckoo) since 2013. He has published two collections of haiku, *Yomo* and *Keikoku*. Inoue was born in Nirasaki City, Yamanashi, Japan in 1952.

ZITA IZSÓ's first collection, *Tengerlakó* (Sea Dweller), won the 2012 Gérecz Attila Prize for Best Debut Book. Her third collection is *Éjszakai földet érés* (Nighttime Earth Arrival).

MARGIT KAFFKA was a Hungarian poet and novelist, born in 1880. She was a member of the first generation of *Nyugat* writers and considered one of the most influential female writers of her day. She died in 1918 of Spanish Influenza.

AGOTA KRISTOF (1935–2011), a Hungarian-born Swiss author, is best known for *The Notebook*, the first part of a trilogy about the brutalities of war. Her Hungarian poems are included in *Clous*, (Editions Zoé, 2016)

TOM KUHN teaches German at St Hugh's College, Oxford, where he is a Fellow. He is the general editor of the English Brecht edition with Bloomsbury-Methuen Drama.

ZAFFAR KUNIAL was born in Birmingham and lives in Hebden Bridge, West Yorkshire. His first full poetry collection, *Us*, was published by Faber & Faber in 2018.

JÚLIA LÁZÁR has published four volumes of poetry: *Fingerprints*, *Unknown, Still* and *Stoneface,* and numerous translations from English including E.M. Forster, George Orwell, Sylvia Plath and Ted Hughes.

BRIAN MCCLEAN is a British-born translator who moved to Hungary in 1977. He translates Hungarian into English, mainly academic texts but occasionally poetry.

CHRIS MCCABE's most recent collection is *Speculatrix* (Penned in the Margins). His first novel, *Dedalus,* has just been published by Henningham Family Press.

MARTHA MEGA is a poet, performer, theatre director, and musician from Mexico City. She runs the company *Sí o Sí Teatro* and has recently released the poetry book *Vergüenza* (Shame), on Mantarraya Ediciones.

MÓNIKA MESTERHÁZI (Budapest, 1967) is a poet, essayist and freelance literary translator. She has published four books of poetry, and is putting together a book of essays on Hungarian poetry, from 20th century classics to contemporaries.

ILKA MESZELY is an illlustrator based in Budapest. Follow her on Instagram @ilkameszley

KATRINA NAOMI's most recent collection is *The Way the Crocodile Taught Me* (Seren, 2016). *Typhoon Etiquette,* a pamphlet inspired by Japan, is forthcoming with Verve Poetry Press in April 2019. www.katrinanaomi.co.uk

SAMIRA NEGROUCHE was born in 1980 in Algiers where she still lives. She trained as a doctor but has privileged her work as a poet and translator – from Arabic to French – for several years. Her books include: *Le Jazz des oliviers* (2010) and *Six arbres de fortune autour de ma baignoire* (2017).

ANDRÁS PETŐCZ is a poet, critic, novelist, and children's author. His awards include an Attila József Prize, the Robert Graves Prize, the Sándor Márai Prize and a UNESCO-Aschberg Laureateship.

SÁNDOR PETŐFI (1823–1849) was born in the town of Kiskörös. He is one of Hungary's most significant Romantic poets and his poem 'National Song' captured the spirit of the Hungarian Revolution in 1848.

GABI REIGH emigrated from Romania to England in her teens. She won the Stephen Spender prize in 2017 and has translated *Poems of Light* by Lucian Blaga and *The Town with Acacia Trees* by Mihail Sebastian.

MANZANARES DE LA ROSA is a radio producer, editor, translator and film programmer from the Yucatán peninsula, in México. He's the founder of 4913, a multi-disciplinary initiative to highlight the work of artists from marginalized, mainly indigenous communities.

LESLEY SAUNDERS, herself a much-published poet, won the 2016 Stephen Spender Trust open award for poetry in translation with her version of Horta's 'Poema'.

MÁRTON SIMON's debut collection, *Dalok a magasföldszintről* (Songs from the High Ground Floor), containing this poem, appeared 2010. His latest collection, *Rókák Esküvője* (Fox Wedding), is forthcoming October 2018.

VERENA STEFAN (1947–2017) was a Swiss-born feminist and writer living in Germany, and later Canada. Her first book *Häutungen*, based on her experiences living in Berlin, became a classic.

GEORGE SZIRTES's most recent book is *Mapping the Delta* (2016). He was awarded the T S Eliot Prize for *Reel* (2004) and has been twice shortlisted since.

ATTILA TÁRNOK is a university lecturer and literary translator. He graduated from the University of Toronto and holds a PhD in Postcolonial Literature.

D SYME-TAYLOR is a writer, student, and translator. She was the winner Oxford University's Newdigate Prize for Poetry in 2013.

KRISZTINA TÓTH (b. 1967) studied sculpture and literature in Budapest, where she now lives. The author of ten books of poetry and seven of prose, her play *Pokémon go*, a grotesque portrayal of Central European realities today, is currently running in Budapest.

JIM TUCKER is a former classical philologist who translates from German, Hungarian, French, and Italian. He lives in Budapest.

FRANCOIS VILLON was born in Paris in 1431 and disappeared from history in 1462. His major works are *The Legacy* and *The Testament*.

ROSA WALLING-WEFELMEYER is one of New Writing North and The Poetry School's 2017/18 New North Poets.

CHRISTOPHER WHYTE translates poetry mainly from Russian and Hungarian into English and Scottish Gaelic, but writes his own poetry exclusively in Scottish Gaelic. His complete English version of Marina Tsvetaeva's *After Russia* (1928) has just been published by Shearsman.

CHRISSY WILLIAMS is a poet, editor and tutor based in London. Her first collection *BEAR* was published in 2017 by Bloodaxe Books.

JL WILLIAMS' books include *Condition of Fire*, *Locust and Marlin* and *After Economy* (Shearsman). She seeks to expand dialogue through writing across languages, perspectives and forms. www.jlwilliamspoetry.co.uk

PÉTER ZÁVADA is a poet and playwright born in Budapest. His first collection of poems appeared in 2012; his second, *Mész*, followed in 2015, and his third, *Roncs szélárnyékban* in 2017.